PRAISE HACKING CLASSROOM MANAGEMENT

Hollywood might not make a movie about you, even if you read and apply every suggestion in this book, but you and your students are much more likely to feel like classroom stars because of it. Mike writes from experience; he's learned, sometimes the hard way, what works and what doesn't, and he shares those lessons in this fine little book. The book is loaded with specific, easy-to-apply suggestions that will help any teacher create and maintain a classroom where students treat one another with respect, and where they learn.

CHRIS CROWE, ENGLISH PROFESSOR AT BYU, PAST PRESIDENT OF ALAN, AUTHOR OF *DEATH COMING UP THE HILL*, *GETTING AWAY WITH MURDER: THE TRUE STORY OF THE EMMETT TILL CASE*; *MISSISSIPPI TRIAL, 1955*; AND MANY OTHER YA BOOKS

Mike Roberts has brought to life a classroom management guidebook that is practical, inspirational, and much needed. As we all know, if you don't have classroom management, you ain't got squat! No matter what grade you teach, there's something of great value inside. Two Big Thumbs UP!

ALAN SITOMER, CA TEACHER OF THE YEAR AWARD WINNER, AUTHOR *SHORT WRITES*

This is the book I wish I had when I first walked into my 7th grade English/Language Arts classroom 18 years ago. Mike Roberts has captured perfectly what teachers need to know and be able to do in order to build rapport with students so they will be open and receptive to learning. This easy-to-read text includes "What You Can Do Tomorrow" sections in each chapter for the desperate teacher who needs quick tips to get back on course, as well as "Full Implementation" outlines for more in-depth, year-long future planning. Most importantly, these ideas are practical, cost effective and easy to implement. As a veteran teacher, I would use this book to remind me why I wanted to teach in the first place and how to get back in touch with principles and practices that will lessen student resistance, increase student learning, and reinvigorate my own joy and satisfaction in teaching.

MARIA GRIFFIN, PROGRAM MANAGER OF TRANSITION TO TEACHING AT SALT LAKE COMMUNITY COLLEGE

Hacking Classroom Management is good for teachers at the beginning, in the middle, and at the end of the teaching journey. Following practical hacks and drawing from both anecdote and film, Roberts offers novel approaches to common concerns inside and outside of the classroom. Whether it is the start of a new year, meeting a new student group, planning for the day, or the unit, Roberts offers a multitude of hacks ready to roll into the room.

PAUL HANKINS, AP ENGLISH LANGUAGE/COMPOSITION TEACHER AT SILVER CREEK HS IN FLOYDS KNOB, INDIANA

Mike Roberts is a teacher of immense energy and creativity. In this refreshing book, he applies his talents to creating a classroom culture that promotes deep engagement and joy in service of understanding, independence and expertise. While reading, I was reminded of Vygotsky's injunction that all teaching and learning are relational and occur in relationship. This book both invites you and shows you how to use various tools to create a positive classroom culture of transformation. I found it immensely fun and illuminating to read!

JEFFERY D. WILHELM, DISTINGUISHED PROFESSOR OF ENGLISH EDUCATION AT BOISE STATE UNIVERSITY, AUTHOR OF *ENGAGING READERS AND WRITERS WITH INQUIRY*, *DIVING DEEP INTO NONFICTION*, AND 35 OTHER BOOKS ON LITERACY

This quick read is a must for all teachers—new teachers, veteran teachers, and those in-between. The hacks for classroom management presented here are practical, useful, and fun. Mike Roberts understands teaching and learning well. This book is awesome. Read it!

JOCELYN GUKEISEN, MIDDLE SCHOOL DIRECTOR AT THE McGILLIS SCHOOL IN SALT LAKE CITY

HACKING
CLASSROOM
MANAGEMENT

10 Ideas To Help You Become the Type of Teacher They Make Movies About

HACK
Learning
SERIES

MIKE
ROBERTS

Hacking Classroom Management
© 2017 by Times 10 Publications

These books are available at special discounts when purchased in quantity for use as premiums, promotions, fundraising, and educational use. For inquiries and details, contact us at 10publications.com.

Published by Times 10
Highland Heights, OH
10publications.com

Project Management by Rebecca Morris and Kelly Schuknecht
Cover Design by Tracey Henterly
Interior Design by Steven Plummer
Editing by Jennifer Jas
Proofreading by Carrie White-Parrish
Creative consulting by Mike Doutt

Library of Congress Cataloging-in-Publication Data is available.

Paperback ISBN: 978-0-9985705-8-7

First Printing: December, 2017
Second Printing: May, 2021
Third Printing: Mar, 2023

CONTENTS

THIS TEACHING THING IS KIND OF HARD

INTRODUCTION

WE'VE ALL SEEN the movies. You know, the ones with *that* teacher. The mentor who inspires students to reach new heights. The guru who somehow manages to create a classroom environment where students want to learn not for the sake of the grade, but rather for the respect of the teacher. The educational sage who instills in students not only a mastery of the subject, but also a clear understanding of life. Yeah, those movies.

Whether it was decades of students coming back to pay homage to Mr. Holland, students standing on their desks to let Mr. Keating know that they finally understood his message, or students exceeding expectations on their AP exams as a result of Mr. Escalante's dedication, those movie teachers always seemed to get their students to perform at their highest potential.

Now if we are being honest, we all originally set out to be one of those teachers. We were excited as we sat through our methods courses. We loved telling our friends stories from student teaching. And there was a sense of pride in telling people, when asked what we do for a living, that, "I am a teacher." But then, usually within the first few months of having our own classrooms, reality kicked in. Overcrowded classrooms, grade-obsessed parents, and overbearing administrators all started to cloud our dreams. Add to this a lack of funding, constant grading, and unmotivated students (among *numerous* other things), and, well, you get the idea.

But what if I were to tell you that there is a way, even with those obstacles staring you down, that you could still become one of those movie-type teachers? And what if I said that all this could be accomplished courtesy of a few easy-to-implement classroom management hacks? Even better, what if these concepts were modeled for you through both real-world scenarios and via some of the best teachers from the past thirty years of cinema? Would you be interested?

BUT I'VE ALREADY TAKEN A CLASSROOM MANAGEMENT CLASS

Now before I go on, let's clarify exactly what this book is and isn't about. First, while this *is* a classroom management book, it's not going to be very useful if you are looking for reactive strategies to help solve your behavioral problems *after* they have already happened. If that fire is already ablaze within your class, you're probably not going to find your extinguisher within these pages.

Instead, the hacks presented here tend to be more proactive. In my experience, the best way to manage the classroom environment is to create a learning atmosphere where students know that they are appreciated, where they are actively engaged in the learning, and where they can have (prepare to gasp!) fun in the process. Simply put, my goal is to provide you with ten quick and easy management hacks that will make your classroom the place to be for *all* your students.

WILL I HAVE TO CHANGE MY CURRICULUM FOR THIS?

Have you ever been to a conference session or a professional development day and walked out with absolutely nothing that was of use to you or your students? Sure, you might have been given some stats and theory on the topic (and, if you're lucky, maybe even a copy of the PowerPoint), but as far as a takeaway that was actually *useful* within your classroom, you came away with zilch. Yeah, I've been to those, too. After nearly twenty years of attending and presenting at various conferences, a few things have become clear to me.

Teachers want resources that can be implemented into their current curriculum. As the majority of teachers will tell you, time is a *very* valuable commodity. And while there are a bunch of really great teaching resources out there, the problem is that many of them require adjusting (or completely overhauling) your current curriculum in order to implement the ideas. Now if you're like me, I really don't want to scrap years of classroom-tested lesson plans just to keep up with the latest educational trend.

It is for this very reason that the majority of the hacks presented here can be incorporated within the context of what you already do. And yes, while some will require more time than others, overall, these hacks are simple and straightforward to execute. After all, the purpose of this book is not to add a pile of new responsibilities to your teaching plate, but rather to help you incorporate some simple, effective, and long-lasting classroom management hacks that enhance what you already successfully do.

Teachers know that processes proven to work in actual classrooms hold much more merit than research conducted on a select group of students. When I started thinking about writing this book, my goal was to create a resource that would be useful to *all* teachers. Again, there are plenty of methodology books out there targeted to a particular grade level or subject matter, but to me, great teaching is great teaching. Because of this, I wanted to create something that provided a series of ready-to-go classroom management strategies that teachers could use regardless of grade level, subject taught, or school environment.

Even still, these hacks can serve as a starting point, and they may require a little tweaking for these concepts to fit with your particular audience. There is no one-size-fits-all system in education. By putting your own spin on these hacks, you will ultimately determine their success. That said, after having tested each of these classroom management ideas in an actual classroom with real students over multiple school years, I am confident that they will be just as effective for you as they have been for me.

Teachers are willing to go above and beyond for the sake of their students, schools, and communities. Obtaining resources is becoming more and more of a challenge with each passing year, and it's not uncommon for teachers to spend their own money in order for their students to have basic classroom supplies. Because of this, I wanted to make sure these hacks could be incorporated with very little (if any) added expense. And again, certain elements discussed within these pages naturally come with expenses (standing desks, field trips, guest speakers), but generally speaking, all it takes to implement most of these ideas is a little planning and the willingness to try.

To be a great teacher—and I'm talking about the type of teacher they make movies about—requires more than simply showing up and doing your job. I'm sure you can think of plenty of decent teachers at your school who know their content and teach their students day in and day out. But those who take their teaching to the next level flip this approach. Movie-worthy teachers know their students and teach their content. In doing so, they realize the positive impact of making personal connections with their students. And it is this connection, combined with simple management strategies, which leads to an effectively managed classroom. Classroom management isn't about knowing what to do after things fall apart, but rather it is about managing the classroom environment in a way that prevents things from melting down.

Simply put, no matter how well you know your content, your class won't reach its full potential until you develop an engaging approach to classroom management, and these hacks will help you do just that. This book offers resources to implement into your current curriculum, processes proven to work in actual classrooms, and simple ideas to help you become even more of a star teacher than you already are, as you go above and beyond for your students!

Hack Learning loyalists will recognize the structure of the book, including The Problem, The Hack, What You Can Do Tomorrow, A Blueprint for Full Implementation, Overcoming Pushback, and The Hack in Action. As an added bonus, each Hack (chapter) includes a helpful visual called "Behind the Scenes." This feature shows you examples, pictures, or prompts to help you fully understand what the hack looks and feels like. I invite you to borrow these ideas outright or use them as springboards to inspire your own adaptations. Each chapter concludes with a final boost of motivation by describing a movie teacher who exemplifies that particular hack.

REMEMBER, IT'S A CLASSROOM, NOT BOOT CAMP

Think of It as Classroom Management 2.0

HACK 1

Control leads to compliance; autonomy leads to engagement.
— DANIEL PINK, AUTHOR

THE PROBLEM: TEACHERS START THE YEAR WITH "NO"

AH, YES—THE FIRST day of class. That special time of the year when everything starts fresh. New students. New ideas. New opportunities. And the same old first day routine. If you are like many teachers, the first day of class, whether it be the beginning of the year, a quarter, or a semester, is often spent going through introductions, expectations, and rules. And while the introductions generally start things off on the right foot, momentum begins to slip a bit once you start talking about expectations. And by the time you hit the rules, well, that's where the "no" rainstorm really opens up.

- No chewing gum.

- No eating or drinking in class.

- No going to the bathroom without permission.

- No talking without raising your hand.

- No cheating.

- No cell phones.

- No inappropriate/disrespectful language.

- No being out of dress code.

Whew! And those are just the basics.

Now I don't know about you, but nothing gets me pumped up like being given a list of what I *can't* do! While there is an argument for being firm and laying the foundation for the rules right off the bat, there is also something to be said about overdoing it. And from my experience, if you go overboard with the rules early on, there might not be a lifeboat that can save you when you need it.

 As you begin to redistribute the power of the class in ways that are more student-centered, your students will become much more invested in wanting all aspects of the class to succeed.

For far too long now, traditional thoughts about classroom management have stressed the need for teachers to hold complete control over the classroom. The problem with this, however, is that effective classroom management isn't about control. It's about understanding the needs of your students. So whereas the outdated 1.0 version of classroom management focused on the teacher retaining power over the students, the new 2.0 version provides students with the opportunity to take some ownership in the daily happenings within the classroom. So rather than starting the year by telling students what *isn't* allowed, classroom management 2.0 provides students with a little more freedom in regard to what *is* permitted. Essentially, with just a few minor tweaks to what you already do, this hack will transform the basic elements of your classroom management routine into processes that benefit both you and your students.

THE HACK: REMEMBER, IT'S A CLASSROOM, NOT BOOT CAMP

Classroom management 2.0 is a concept based around the idea that students should be treated a little less like soldiers and a little more like people. As teachers, we ask a great deal of our students each and every day, and as a show of good faith, we should find little ways where we can loosen the chokehold of control and give them an opportunity to have a voice in what their class will look like. By providing them this freedom, you are also giving them the opportunity to take more ownership in the class. This, in turn, will result in a more engaged and attentive class.

Now, I am by no means suggesting that you let the inmates run the prison. You are still the one in charge of the room. However, I am recommending that you not only get input from your students regarding the day-to-day rules and procedures, but also alter some of your tried-and-true classroom management strategies. In fact, I'm going after two of the classics right off the bat!

Seating charts. The golden oldie of classroom management 1.0! Rather than assigning students seats on the first day, give them the opportunity to sit where they want. Then, as you are discussing other rules and procedures, let them know that they are welcome to sit where they want as long as they are able to responsibly handle the situation. This gives them a sense of ownership about it, and rather than fighting against the seating chart, they will fight for the seating chart. And if certain students are unable to properly cope with this freedom, talk to those students individually and come up with a consequence that they can agree on. But please, *never* punish the entire class by taking this privilege away (see "Don't punish the entire class" in the Blueprint section of this chapter) based on one or two problematic students.

Now before you get all worried that this will make your class chaotic, rest assured that if your class is like mine, your students will tend to sit in the same general location every day, even without being told to. Students like routine, and they will fall into their own system more easily if you allow them to take a little ownership of the situation.

Asking to go to the bathroom. Can we please let this one go? Seriously, when was the last time you had to publicly ask if you could go to the bathroom? I'm guessing it was when you were in school. To put an end to this, as a class, come up with a nonverbal signal that students give you when they need to go to the bathroom. In my class, students simply point to the door when nature calls. I then give a quick nod to let them know that I am aware they are leaving, and off they go. Another simple method is to have a sign-out sheet that students sign whenever they leave. This can be as simple as a pen and paper next to the door.

Both methods save the students the embarrassment of making a public announcement, and it allows you as the teacher to keep the momentum of class flowing. And while it might not sound like much, giving your class this type of respect shows that you are willing to look at them as people, and in return, they will reflect that respect through appropriate in-class behavior.

While simple in nature, allowing your class more freedom

regarding your seating chart and bathroom policy signals a sign of good faith to your students. Ultimately, you are building a foundation of trust and respect—two key elements of an effectively run classroom.

WHAT YOU CAN DO TOMORROW

In addition to saying goodbye to the traditional seating chart and bathroom routine, here are a few more simple ideas that will solidify your classroom management by adding clarity and student responsibility to your routines.

- **REVIEW YOUR RULES.** I often kept certain rules around, not because they were effective and improved my classroom management, but simply because I had always used them. With that in mind, take a few minutes tomorrow and evaluate the effectiveness of each of your rules. I'm guessing that if you *really* look at them, you will discover that a few of them could be dropped without impacting your effectiveness.

- **PUT UP THE DAILY SCHEDULE.** Students like knowing the plan for the day, and putting the class schedule on the board is an easy way to keep them in the loop. And you don't necessarily need to be super specific with this; a general overview is enough. This simple act will help improve classroom management because it allows students to know what is coming up versus leaving them in the dark. Uncertainty often leads to disruptive behavior, and knowing what to expect alleviates this. Plus, as the teacher, this schedule will help you stay on track, eliminating tangents and overdoing a topic (two additional issues that lead to student misbehavior).

• **ELIMINATE COLD CALLING.** Look, I get the logic of this one. You are trying to get everyone involved in the class discussion, and sometimes students need encouragement to participate. But let's be real here—while it's true that cold calling on kids improves the level of student participation, it's crucial to note that it's a *forced* level of engagement. It would be like saying that the draft improved the number of people in the military. Did it accomplish the goal? Yes. Did it get total buy-in from everyone involved? Probably not.

From my experience both as a student and a teacher, this method can backfire if the student that you call on doesn't know the answer to your question. And rather than getting that student engaged in the discussion, you just embarrassed that kid in front of the entire class. The end result is that you negatively impacted your relationship with that student, thus damaging any potential sharing that student might have in the future. The worst part is that while it might work nine times out of ten, that one wrong answer given by the student can erase all nine correct responses in one gigantic swoop. From my perspective, it's just not worth the gamble.

If you truly want to get some of the less-vocal students more involved, front-load the situation by giving them a heads-up after class about what you will be discussing tomorrow, and let them know that you would like to hear their thoughts (see Hack 2). Tell them that they can pick their moments, but when their hands go up, you are going to call on them. This not only gets them involved this one time, but it also establishes trust with them (and perhaps a willingness to answer questions in the future) that will remain throughout the year.

A BLUEPRINT FOR FULL IMPLEMENTATION

Step 1: Commit to letting students be empowered.

It's one thing to say you are transferring some of the power of the class to the students, but it's another to actually do it. This is not as easy as it sounds, and you may fall back to your old ways at times. But just remember that the end goal is to empower your students more in the routines of class, and every time you stumble, get back up and keep moving forward.

Step 2: Frame expectations in a positive tone.

The more rules you have, the more likely students are to break them. So rather than posting a bunch of rules all over your walls, why not establish a few class agreements that encompass the big-ticket behavioral concepts? And instead of posting signs about no swearing, hitting, yelling, or running, why not establish and discuss what appropriate behavior looks like? Putting these ideas into a positive context will let students know what they *should* be doing, rather than constantly telling them what they *shouldn't* be doing. (See Act 1: It's All in How You Say It.)

It's All In How You Say It

INSTEAD OF THIS....	SAY THIS...
"You must sit in your assigned seat..."	"Pick a seat where you will be the most productive with your time."
"You have to ask permission in order to go to the bathroom..."	"If you have to go to the bathroom, just autograph the sign-out sheet so I know where you are."
"Everyone is expected to participate, so be ready to be called on at any time..."	"The expectation is that everyone participates, so make sure you jump in when you have something good to say."
"No swearing or bad language..."	"Have a little class when you speak."
"I will wait for your attention..."	"Ladies and gentleman, can I please have your attention?"
"No cell phones..."	"You have your phones with you all day, and you only get to see me for an hour. Plus, they will only distract you from all the awesome stuff we are going to be doing."
"No cheating..."	"Trust me, your integrity isn't worth a point or two on a quiz."

Behind the Scenes Act 1: It's All in How You Say It

Step 3: Include students in the implementation of rules and procedures.

Letting students have a voice in the rules and procedures of your class will greatly improve the odds of these concepts lasting throughout the course of the year. By providing them with a say in the rules, it will make it easier to refer back to what "we" (the class) came up with as a guideline for class, rather than what "I" (the teacher) assigned if/when things start to fall apart.

Step 4: Don't punish the entire class.

As a general rule, the vast majority of your students listen and behave themselves during class—although there are always exceptions. Because of this, class punishments really can have a negative impact on the atmosphere. If a student misbehaves, deal with that student individually. And if you aren't sure who caused the infraction, lay low until you have a chance to investigate and make an informed decision. If you panic and punish the entire class, you're isolating yourself from a large percentage of innocent students. Plus, if you start interrogating students and looking for information, you are often unintentionally pitting students against one another. This is a surefire way to break up any trust you've built within your class, and as a result, rather than eliminating issues, you may be creating them.

Step 5: Stop sharing the class average.

While sharing the class average on tests and assignments might seem harmless, in reality, it sets students up to compare themselves to one another. Once grades get involved, students tend to get competitive, and by promoting what "average" looks like, they will naturally compare themselves against that score.

An easy solution is to ask students to reflect on their own grades to see if they represent their best efforts (see Hack 7). This allows your class to think about what they did in comparison to *themselves* versus comparing their score to what everyone *else* earned. I always tell my students that the only score they should be concerned with is their own. Besides, your students shouldn't strive for mediocrity, and that's exactly the measurement you are asking them to compare themselves against when you post the class average.

Step 6: Change as needed.

Like most everything else about teaching, be ready to adapt these concepts. In a perfect world, all of these classroom management strategies would fit perfectly with your learning community. Unfortunately, I have yet to see a perfect school. Find what works for both you and your class, and build from there.

OVERCOMING PUSHBACK

Classroom management 2.0 is probably a bit different than what you've always done. But that's the point! If you still need convincing, however, here are a few responses for the naysayers:

I already have a system that works. Look, I get it. You have a system in place that works perfectly fine for you and your students. But what if trying some of these ideas resulted in a *better* system? Don't you think it would be worth a try? For example, when a student tells you that he has a "method" for something that you are doing in class, are you content to let him use his usual method, or do you encourage him to try what you know has worked with other students to see if it can improve his results? The way I see it, you will never know which style works best until you try a few and have a basis for comparison. Besides, what do you really have to lose by trying these out for a week or two?

What about the students who abuse the bathroom privilege? This one is easy: What do you currently do about students who abuse the bathroom privilege? Do that! In my class, we discuss the bathroom policy at the beginning of the year, and we establish a general idea for what seems like an appropriate number of times to leave class for the bathroom and water breaks per trimester. History has shown that most students can easily limit this to two times or less per trimester. But, like most rules, there are always students out there who want to see how much they can get away with, so they push that recommended limit.

When that happens, I let the students know that I have noticed them leaving fairly often, and I will ask if there are any issues that I need to be made aware of. (There may be times when students have extenuating situations that require them to leave class more frequently. These situations should be treated individually, and are often included in students' accommodation plans.) In most cases, simply letting students know that you are aware is enough to end the problem. But just in case, I remind them to use the passing time to visit the bathroom when possible, rather than class time. In essence, all this new method is doing is cutting out the public announcement piece. Whatever rules you've previously established about using the bathroom are still in play.

My students will mess around without a seating chart. This is a common concern, but I bet if you really think about it, you will realize that most of us use a seating chart primarily to keep one or two students in check. If that's the case, is it really fair to punish the entire class based on the actions of a couple students? And again, if students are aware of the consequences that come with misbehaving (losing the privilege of free seating), that alone will keep many of them from taking advantage of the situation. Besides, if it totally blows up (which I doubt will happen), you can always break out the seating chart later.

But if I don't cold call on students, they won't participate. This is the standard argument I hear from teachers when I propose the no-cold-calling method. If this is truly the case, you may need to reassess your relationship with your students. If the relationship is built on trust and respect, your students should be willing to share their ideas, even when possibly wrong. Plus, if you have established and modeled risk-taking as part of your class, your students will take more chances on speaking up.

The other argument I often hear is when a teacher says that the same three kids answer all the questions, so they use cold calling as a way to get more students involved. Again, if you have established a learning-friendly atmosphere where students are challenged to share their thoughts, all you have to do is say, "I appreciate these hands that are up, but I want to see some new hands up in the air." That simple piece of encouragement is usually enough to get a second wave of students involved in the conversation. These are the students who are generally already engaged in the class, but just need a little prompting to share. This gives them the autonomy to participate versus being forced into participating, and autonomy will lead to greater responsibility.

Finally, if you ask a question and get no volunteers, here are two more ideas. First, let students do a turn-n-talk (see Hack 4) to discuss their ideas with classmates. Giving them a minute or two to digest the question usually is enough to get students to engage. If that doesn't work, then maybe you didn't ask a very good question! It happens, but at the same time, it's not fair to blame your students for not answering a question that they might not understand. Try rephrasing the question.

THE HACK IN ACTION

When middle school Chinese teacher Tyler Tanner initially started teaching, he shared a set of eleven rules that students should follow. He says, "It was a running joke in my class that these were the Eleven Commandments." But as he gained experience, Tanner soon realized that he was going overboard regarding what his students could and couldn't do. "Today, my rules are simple: Be cool to each other and always give your best effort." And rather than explaining to his class what "being cool" means, Tanner instead allows his students to share their thoughts on what that does or does not look like. "If the students do something they shouldn't, all I have to say is, 'Are you being cool to each other?' If they aren't, they will typically stop, and oftentimes even apologize for their behavior."

In addition to limiting his rules, Tanner has implemented many procedural elements that provide students with increased autonomy. "In my class, I don't believe in using a seating chart. Where students sit doesn't matter to me as long as they are being respectful and productive. Plus, allowing students the freedom to sit where they want makes them *want* to behave so that the seats aren't assigned." Additionally, he has also stopped the cold-calling approach. In conjunction with the "Always give your best effort" rule, he discovered that students like to be part of the class, and if they are prepared and giving their best effort, this eliminates the need to cold call on students.

"I have found that if you treat the students as you would want to be treated, there are a lot less behavioral issues. If you set the bar high and treat them accordingly, you will be surprised how many of them are willing to meet you at that level."

In the movie *Lean on Me*, Principal Joe Clark knew he had to help his school rise above its gang and narcotics problems before he could focus on improving state exam scores. He did this by showing students that he, along with the entire school community, was invested in their success.

Just before the state exams, he announced to a room full of students, "We sink, we swim, we rise, we fall, we meet our fate together!" He established a system where everyone became a stakeholder in the success, or failure, of the school, and he refused to let good enough be *good enough*. He focused on what is truly important (improving student lives), and his students repaid him by putting forth their best efforts in and out of class. Principal Clark gave them a voice in the educational process, while still maintaining high standards (see Hack 2).

By giving your students a little leeway with the classic rules of classroom management (seating chart, bathroom breaks), and tweaking how you run the day-to-day routines (no more cold calling, mass class punishments, sharing the class average), you can dramatically improve the engagement, learning, and relationships. As you begin to redistribute the power of the class in ways that are more student-centered, your students will become more invested in wanting all aspects of the class to succeed.

EXPECT THEIR BEST (IN AND OUT OF THE CLASSROOM)

Setting and Modeling High Expectations

HACK 2

For most of us the problem isn't that we aim too high and fail – it's just the opposite – we aim too low and succeed.
— SIR KEN ROBINSON, AUTHOR AND EDUCATIONAL ADVISOR

THE PROBLEM: TEACHERS LET A STUDENT'S PAST DETERMINE THE PRESENT

LETTING GO OF the past is tough. When I was in ninth grade, I had a sweet acid-washed jacket. I mean, I wore that thing everywhere! Whether at school, a party, or a sporting event—if I was there, I was rocking my jacket. Problem was, purchasing that jacket also coincided with me going through a growth spurt, and by the time I was midway through my sophomore year, my jacket no longer fit. Throw in the fact that the acid-washed craze fizzled out as quickly as it started, and it makes perfect sense that I would have gotten rid of it. But I just couldn't bring myself to do it. And for whatever reason, rather than donating the jacket to Goodwill, I let it sit in my closet for *years*! Yep, it wasn't until I left for college that I was finally able to pull the plug on that beauty.

I'm not really sure why I kept that jacket around for so long. Maybe it was comforting to know the history behind it. After all, I knew where it came from, what it had been through, and all the stories connected with it. Maybe, in some weird way, seeing it hanging there served as a reminder of how life used to be. While I'll be the first to admit there is something to be said for nostalgia, sometimes knowing *too much* about the past can have a downside. And this is especially true when it comes to your students.

 Regardless of how often you tell your students that you trust them, find opportunities to *show* that you trust them.

Too often, when we see a student's IEP, the list of accommodations, and the below-average test scores, we instantly lower our expectations. In fact, sometimes there isn't even a file that causes us to do this. It can be as simple as a student being related to one of your former students. And when this happens, rather than challenging these students to reach new heights, we often allow them to settle for a level of success that is far below their potential. After all, there's no way a student could change from one year to the next, right?

This hack asks you to turn the tables on the status quo by challenging you to establish, and model, high expectations for your students. And rather than simply letting your students' past determine their present, the ideas presented here allow your students' potential to create their future.

THE HACK: EXPECT THEIR BEST (IN AND OUT OF THE CLASSROOM)

I love the first day of school. Teachers show up in their nicest outfits, feeling relaxed from summer vacation, students are bright-eyed and ready to learn, and your room smells fresher than it will the rest of the year. You relish getting to know your students, and you are sure that they will find more success in your class than in any other class they have ever taken. It's a magical time!

Now fast forward to the week before winter break. The relaxed feelings of summer have been replaced with three months of stress, your once-eager students now drag themselves to class, and your room smells like a mixture of feet and body odor. And your wardrobe? Let's just say that your first-day outfit has been replaced by jeans and a T-shirt that you may or may not have worn yesterday. So the question that begs to be asked is: Where did all that first-day optimism go?

If you're like many teachers, the day-to-day problems of school often impact the attitude that we bring to the classroom. As a result, all the little issues that arise over the course of a school year end up shattering our best of intentions. This approach is somewhat backwards, if you ask me. Rather than letting the school's problems impact your attitude, you should instead let your attitude shape the actions of school. Let me explain.

When the year starts, we (hopefully) set the bar high with regard to classroom expectations. We let our students know what to do to find success, and we hope (and sometimes pray) that it will all work out. We trust them, both in and out of class, to do what's right. But as many of you know, things rarely work out perfectly, and little by little, those high expectations begin to crack. One student forgets to turn in a homework assignment. Another is constantly showing up late. A third gets caught cheating. And that one kid—yeah, he's driving you crazy! But rather than addressing these issues as they arise and re-establishing that behaviors like these aren't acceptable, it just becomes easier for both you and the students to let the high expectations slide. Once that happens, lowering the bar becomes the new norm.

The key ingredient to making this hack a success is to bring the excitement and optimism that you display on the first day to every class you teach. And on those occasions when students don't live up to expectations, hold them accountable for their actions. Classroom management and high expectations go hand-in-hand, and when one falters, the other is soon to follow. From my experience, students feed off the energy and attitude of the teacher, and you'll want to consistently demand the best from your students. If they see you "bring it" every day, and you are clear about your expectation for them to do the same, you will be amazed at the high standards they can attain. And before too long, those high expectations become the new norm.

WHAT YOU CAN DO TOMORROW

While it is obviously best to set clear expectations at the beginning of each school year, there are valuable steps that can be implemented at any point. Each of the following strategies is a simple and effective method that can be immediately added to help you establish high expectations.

- **START EACH CLASS WITH A SMILE**. As easy as this sounds, this simple act will set the tone for the rest of your class. If your students see that you're in a good mood, they will feed off the vibe you're sending out. A positive mood generally relates to fewer discipline infractions, and this results in more smiles. And so the cycle begins.

- **TELL YOUR STUDENTS YOU EXPECT THEIR BEST ON A DAILY BASIS.** Over the course of my career, there have been times when my students have struggled on an assignment, not because it was too difficult, but because my directions were not clear and understandable. The same holds true with regard to behavior. When addressing expectations, explicitly teach and model the behaviors you want to see in your students. Don't assume they know what you mean—show them!

- **DRESS UP.** I have a mantra that says, "Look good. Feel good. Do good." I don't know the science behind it, but I do know that when I dress up, my expectations (for myself and my students) are higher than normal. Plus, teachers often talk about wanting to be treated as professionals, and for this to happen, we need to dress accordingly.

  I also use this philosophy with my students. I tell them that, as a general rule, they will get dressed up for all the big occasions in their lives (graduations, weddings, award ceremonies, funerals). I also let them know that unit tests and presentations in my class are big occasions, and that they should dress up on those days. And yes, before you ask, I do notice an improvement in their behavior on those days!

- **ASK YOUR STUDENTS TO MAKE YOU PROUD.** I'm a big believer that all students truly want to succeed. I also believe that, despite what the news might say, students still have a great deal of respect for their teachers. That's why I blend these two concepts together on a regular basis by asking my students to make me proud through their behavior and effort. By simply letting students know that you expect their absolute best, you will offset many of the classroom management issues (tardiness, disrespectful behavior, disengagement).

- **THANK YOUR CLASS AT THE END OF THE PERIOD.** Like the smile at the beginning, ending class with a "thank you" shows your class that you appreciate their time and that you value the thoughts they shared. Even better, give them high fives, fist bumps, or personalized handshakes on their way out the door (see Hack 9). Again, it's important to model the behavior you want to see, and the more you thank them, the more they will reciprocate.

A BLUEPRINT FOR FULL IMPLEMENTATION

Step 1: Clearly articulate your expectations on day one.

The sooner you can establish the expectations of your class, the better off you and your class will be. While I am not suggesting that you bombard your students with a bunch of rules as soon as they walk in the door (see Hack 1), I am recommending that you let your students know that you expect their absolute best, both in and out of the classroom, from day one.

Step 2: Hold all students to high expectations.

Once the expectations have been established, consistently reinforce them. However, the expectations for each student will be different based on ability and situation. It's crucial to remember that the level of expectation should be challenging, because the point of having high expectations is to push students to reach new heights.

Step 3: Differentiate often.

Differentiation is a key element to this hack. What differentiation means is rather than asking students to conform to a one-size-fits-all assignment, you make sure that there are a wide range of options available that play to the strengths of the various students within your class. Differentiation should include offering a variety of reading options, project choices, and assessment opportunities. And no, this does not mean that you need to lower your expectations for students. What it means is that you understand how to get the *most* out of each of your students. Simply put, differentiation gives your students a chance to participate in the learning in a way that is best suited to their individual learning needs.

Step 4: Model what you want to see from your students.

This is perhaps the most important step in this Blueprint. It's one thing to tell your students to up their game; it's another to model what this looks like. Actions speak louder than words, and if you are asking your students to show their best, make sure you are following your own advice.

- Want your students to be on time? Be the first one in class.

- Want your students to be respectful? Say please and thank you frequently.

- Want your students to manage their time? Have a structured lesson prepared for each class.

Step 5: Provide reminders and examples.

Early in my career, I would go over expectations during the first few days of class, and I would assume that was enough to cover it for the remainder of the year. Well, needless to say, I was wrong. To get students to commit to the high expectations, provide them with reminders and examples of what those expectations look like and how they can accomplish them. Identify when students are doing well, and don't be afraid to let them know when they aren't carrying their weight.

Step 6: Show your students that you trust them.

Regardless of how often you tell your students that you trust them, find opportunities to *show* that you trust them. Letting them take a test at home or simply asking them if they completed an assignment (rather than having them show you or turn it in) are two simple ways to build a relationship of trust. Once your students know that they have earned your trust, they will do everything possible to maintain it.

Step 7: Get feedback from your students.

While it seems obvious, many teachers overlook getting student feedback on these issues. Find out what is working, and build on that. And if it isn't working very well, find out why, and adjust it so everything is clear and understandable for your students. Communication is a key element of this hack, and receiving and providing constant feedback is an essential ingredient to its success. (See Act 2: Teacher Evaluation.)

Teacher Evaluation - Mr. Roberts

Please rate Mr. Roberts on the following topics. (1-low, 5-high)

1	Mr. Roberts comes prepared to class.	1	2	3	4	5
2	Mr. Roberts sets clear expectations.	1	2	3	4	5
3	Mr. Roberts encourages student participation.	1	2	3	4	5
4	Mr. Roberts brings a positive attitude to class.	1	2	3	4	5
5	Mr. Roberts cares about me as a person.	1	2	3	4	5

Please write a response to each of the following questions. Include as many specifics as possible.

What is your favorite part of this class?

What are Mr. Roberts' strengths as a teacher?

What suggestions do you have to make class better?

Please add any additional thoughts you have about this class or Mr. Roberts.

Behind the Scenes Act 2: Teacher Evaluation

OVERCOMING PUSHBACK

Look, there is no denying that holding students to high expectations is more challenging than letting them take the easy way out. And while there will be challenges along the way, movie-type teachers are willing to accept, and overcome, obstacles and questions such as these:

My students already know my expectations. I frequently hear this piece of feedback. But too often, we *assume* our students understand our expectations rather than being absolutely certain that they *know* our expectations. Just like the key concepts taught in your class, the expectations need to be taught, modeled, and performed on a regular basis in order for them to stick.

But what about the students who cheat? A student who wants to cheat on an assignment is going to cheat regardless of whether it's in class or at home. So rather than creating a rule (see Hack 1) based on the *chance* that a small minority of your class *might* cheat, I instead recommend that you focus your expectations on the fact that the vast majority of your class won't cheat or otherwise betray trust.

So how do I let my class know that I expect them not to cheat? I follow these three simple steps.

1. During my explanation of the assignment, I tell them, "I am trusting you not to cheat on this. Don't let me down!"

2. As students pick up the take-home test/assignment, I require them to look me in the eye and say, "I will not cheat." I often repeat my "Don't let me down" comment to each of them individually at this point.

3. When they hand in their work, I ask them to look me in the eye yet again and say, "I promise I did not cheat." As I take the assignment from them, I usually add, "Thank you for being honest with me."

As crazy as it sounds, this approach has substantially reduced the number of students I catch cheating in my class. And let me be clear here: The grades on the take-home exams usually mirror the scores that students receive on their in-class exams, so it's not like students are lying to me about cheating. It's almost as if the trust I place in them outweighs the almighty grade. How's that for a crazy concept?

I don't have fancy clothes to wear to work. As you know, teaching doesn't exactly pay a Wall Street CEO salary. That said, many teachers could upgrade their attire without breaking the bank. You don't need to buy an entirely new wardrobe, but I am suggesting that if you wear jeans and a T-shirt to your class, you may want to class it up and strive for a more professional look.

It's impossible to be happy and positive every day. There's no debating this one. Sometimes, whether because of illness, lack of energy, or just life in general, you are going to have days when you are just off your game a bit. And that's when you fake it. We expect our students to be on every day, and we should hold ourselves to that same standard. So put on some nice clothes, throw on a happy smile, and go model for your students what it means to persevere!

At the same time, when those truly serious occasions arise (like a death in the family), it is absolutely acceptable to let your class know that you are having a tough time. And while I don't recommend dwelling on it, sharing this kind of information can enhance your relationship with your class by creating a bond that just can't be established otherwise.

THE HACK IN ACTION

Eighth-grader Rory Beals says he has experienced classrooms with higher expectations, and those with lower expectations, and reflects on how each impacted his learning and engagement. He says, "I have found that a teacher's expectations of me have a great influence on both my work effort and my desire to do well in class. In every class I have taken, my success in that class can be traced almost exclusively to the expectations set by the teacher." He continues, "In a class with lower standards, I notice students talking over the teacher and ignoring the lesson. In a class with higher expectations, however, I have noticed those same kids being quiet and doing their absolute best to understand the material that is being taught."

Beals says students are well aware when teachers aren't holding up their end of the bargain. "There are many teachers that try to hold high standards for their students who struggle to demonstrate those same expectations themselves. There have been times where a teacher has given my class a test or assignment, and after we turn it in, it takes them weeks to grade it. For some things, such as papers, this makes sense. In other circumstances, like a ten-point quiz, it doesn't make a lot of sense for the teacher to take that long to grade them." His point is that when teachers don't model the behavior they want to see, students begin to question it. "If I can't hold my teachers to high standards, why should they be able to hold me to such high standards?"

Setting and modeling high expectations runs much deeper than any content. It's believing that both you and your students are capable of greatness, regardless of the past, and it's a willingness to work hard to accomplish such greatness.

In the movie *Stand and Deliver*, Jaime Escalante modeled how to hold high expectations for students. During one of the first class periods of the year, Escalante proudly announced, "You're going to work harder here than you've ever worked anywhere else. And the only thing I ask from you is 'ganas.' Desire." Escalante didn't care about his students' pasts. Instead, he focused on the *potential* he saw in each and every one, and they responded via hard work and respect. Later, when questioned about his unique methods and the success of previously low-achieving students, Escalante responded by saying, "Students will rise to the level of expectation." As a result, all eighteen of Escalante's calculus students passed the AP exam—twice.

So the question is: Do you have the 'ganas' to expect the best from your students? To be the type of teacher they make movies about, you'll want to model and maintain high expectations for your students and for yourself.

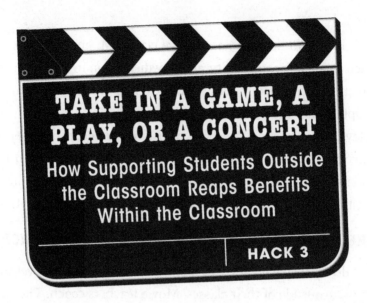

TAKE IN A GAME, A
PLAY, OR A CONCERT

How Supporting Students Outside
the Classroom Reaps Benefits
Within the Classroom

HACK 3

The development occurs through reciprocal give-and-take,
the teacher taking but not being afraid also to give.
— JOHN DEWEY, EDUCATIONAL REFORMER

THE PROBLEM: TEACHERS ONLY SEE
THE STUDENT SIDE OF KIDS

TEACHING TAKES TIME and energy. You have to oversee your curriculum, design an engaging lesson, manage the classroom atmosphere, cover your various duties, attend required meetings, send out miscellaneous emails, and catch up on grading. And that's on an easy day.

Unfortunately, with so much happening every day, it can be tough to get to know your students. I mean, yes, you talk to them. And yes, you hear their thoughts about the ideas presented in class. You might even let them present on topics of their choice every now and then. But in the big picture, it can be a challenge to see your students as more than just students. Yet getting to know your students—and I mean know the persons, not just the students—will build trust that

43

will help you to manage an effective classroom environment. Time is such a valuable commodity, and any disruption in classroom management can completely derail your best-laid plans. And often, these disruptions are the result of a single student.

Have you ever wondered why those movie teachers never seem to struggle with classroom management? There may be an initial problem that starts the movie, but by the time the movie is halfway over, the problem seems to disappear. So how do they do it?

THE HACK: TAKE IN A GAME, A PLAY, OR A CONCERT

They do it, in part, by participating in school-related events that take place outside of their classes. Movie teachers coach. They direct the play. They lead the band or choir. In fact, every good movie teacher that I can think of led or engaged in some kind of extracurricular activity with the students.

The benefit of doing this, of course, is that you get to know your students on a completely different level, and you will often discover a new side to them. This better understanding of your students can then be translated into the in-class relationship. Any bonds you form talking about sports or acting *outside* of class will bleed *into* the classroom. Additionally, when your students see that you're willing to put in the extra time to support them in activities they enjoy, they will become more willing to return the favor during class.

 If your students know that you care about them *outside* of the classroom, they will be more willing to show you that they care about their work *inside* the classroom.

By modeling what it means to be supportive, you set the standard for the behavior you expect from everyone, yourself included.

A new level of respect is established that is difficult to reach within the walls of your classroom. Students look at your class as a place where everyone, teachers and students, *has* to be. Extracurricular events are different in that they are places where people *choose* to be. And every time you decide to show up to one of these events, it will strengthen your relationship with all the students involved.

When you really strip it down to the basic elements, this hack is pretty simple to understand: Supporting your students by attending extracurricular events is an easy and effective way to offset many of the issues that arise in class. It simply shows your students that you care about them beyond your subject area, and that you are willing to give up some of your own time to support them in the activities they enjoy doing. And just so we are clear, while it's ridiculous to attend *all* of the events, it's just as silly to say that you can't attend *any* of the events. Model for your students what it means to be supportive outside the classroom, and they will pay it back within.

WHAT YOU CAN DO TOMORROW

As easy as this sounds, it still requires effort and pre-planning on your part. To help get things rolling, here are a few simple ideas that you can implement immediately.

- **TALK TO YOUR STUDENTS ABOUT UPCOMING EVENTS.** You may not hear about events until after they are over, but if you regularly ask your students what activities they are involved in, you will stay up-to-date on potential events to visit.

- **LOOK AT A SCHOOL CALENDAR AND PUT TOGETHER A PLAN.** If your school is like mine, there is always *something* coming up soon. Take a look at upcoming events, and see which ones work with your schedule, and which ones include your students.

- **CREATE AN EVENT BOARD.** Tape off a portion of your board and label it "Upcoming School Events." Include a section identifying the date, time, event, and location of future activities. This is a great way to keep you posted and help students become engaged with what their classmates are doing, further solidifying the community vibe. (See Act 3: Events.)

EVENTS

DATE	TIME	EVENT	LOCATION
8/31	4:00	VOLLEYBALL	GYM
9/1	4:00	SOCCER	FIELD
9/6	10:00	PICTURE DAY	CAFETERIA
9/15	7:00	DANCE	GYM
9/25	4:00	VOLLEYBALL	GYM
9/29	7:00	DANCE CONCERT	AUDITORIUM

Behind the Scenes Act 3: Events

A BLUEPRINT FOR FULL IMPLEMENTATION

Step 1: Decide if you can do this.

While it's not as daunting as being a coach or a director, attending events still takes up some of your personal time. Decide if you're willing to do it, and if so, if you can put on a happy face while doing it. Students will immediately recognize if you're not enjoying yourself, and just showing up to "check the box" won't strengthen your classroom rapport. If you're going to do it, do it right.

Step 2: Find an event that interests you.

Attending events doesn't have to be something to dread! Find an activity that is of interest to you, because the more engaged you are in the performance, the bigger the return you will get from your students. Plus, if you can connect with them by "talking the talk" of the activity, it will further strengthen your relationship with those who are taking part in the event.

Step 3: Invite colleagues along.

Once you find an event, ask some of your colleagues if they are interested in joining you in attending. In addition to building classroom rapport, school events serve as a great opportunity to solidify collegial relationships. Plus, seeing you hanging out with other teachers is another way for students to see that you have a life outside of your classroom.

Step 4: Attend the event.

Whether it's for fifteen minutes or two hours, the time you spend at the event will be paid back within the classroom. If you really want to add some street cred with your students, sit amongst them in the crowd, and show them a bit of your non-teacher side.

Step 5: Talk about the event the next day in class.

Attending is only the first step. The bigger step is talking with your students about it afterwards. Be sure to heap praise on those who participated, and don't forget to talk with other students who you saw in the crowd about their favorite parts.

Step 6: Start planning your next event.

Attending school events shouldn't be a once-a-year endeavor. For it to have a positive impact on your classroom atmosphere, it should become a regular part of your routine. So check out the calendar, and start planning your next activity.

OVERCOMING PUSHBACK

All right, so I'm not going to lie—this hack is one of the tougher ones for teachers to get on board with. Incorporating new ideas during the workday is one thing; altering time away from school is a whole other issue! Here are some thoughts to address concerns that might arise.

I don't have two hours a day, after school no less, to go to school events. I totally hear you. And the good news is, you don't have to. See, while being a coach or a director requires hours of time—time that many of us can't spare—most of us can manage being a spectator at those events. The fact is, a little effort on your part will go a long way with your students. To make it even easier, you don't even have to watch the whole event. While it's obviously best to stay for the entirety when possible, even making a quick cameo appearance can reap rewards. Simply watching a portion of a game or a play allows you to establish a starting point for a conversation the next day in class. A simple question like, "How did the game end up last night?" or a comment such as, "You did a nice job last night at the play" shows your students that you're interested in their lives beyond the classroom.

You can even turn these occasions into family outings. Younger kids enjoy going to events where they get to see what the older students are doing, and your students will love seeing your children. It's a win-win scenario! While it might not seem like much, this will have a *major* impact on the relationship you have with your students. When students know you care about them as people, they will be much more willing to open up and try new things within your class.

None of the school events interest me. But I bet your students interest you! That is why you are doing this, after all. Although it does help to be interested in the activity itself, that's not the primary reasoning behind why you are spending your time to attend. Try to find a connection with a type of event, such as art shows, music performances, drama performances, dances, sports events or games, or student activities in the community.

But I am their teacher, not their friend. While this is completely true, you can still strive to be supportive of your students as often as you can. Extracurricular activities give you a chance to interact in a friendly, yet professional, manner with your students. You can be friendly and encouraging while being their teacher. And remember, when you attend activities like these, you are still a representative of the school, so act accordingly.

THE HACK IN ACTION

Let's play a little Jeopardy. The answer: Fifty-seven. The question: How many middle school dances that I have chaperoned over the past eighteen years? Yep, you read that correctly: fifty-seven middle school dances!

Now, have I enjoyed all of them? Nah, of course not. I mean, it's two hours of awkward dancing, bad food, and way too much cologne. Seriously, it's a middle school dance. Do I need to say more? But do I feel like each of them helped me to establish positive relationships with my students? Absolutely. When my students see that I am there to support the awkward dancing, to choke down the tasteless food alongside them, and to comment on the need to cut back on the cologne, we connect on a level that just isn't going to happen in Room 202. Plus, when incoming students see me there, it front-loads the relationships we will have if and when they end up in my class.

So while I would never wish fifty-seven middle school dances upon anyone (not even my worst enemy), I am here to say that moments like those have had a tremendous impact in helping me manage and maintain a positive classroom atmosphere.

PE teacher and coach Bobby Kennedy, who has more than twenty years of teaching and coaching experience spanning kindergarten through college, has also experienced these benefits firsthand. He is fully aware of how establishing positive relationships in one area (in his case, coaching soccer) can easily blend into another (the classroom). Coach Kennedy explains, "Because much of what we do as educators revolves around facilitating meaningful connections, I spend a considerable amount of time formally and informally nurturing any opportunity to connect with my students."

In addition to dedicating his time to coaching soccer, Coach Kennedy is also a frequent spectator at various other school events. "When you connect with a student in a way that is not directly linked to the subject or content area you teach, it makes it easier for you as the teacher to have high expectations of that student in the classroom setting. When you see what they are capable of in other areas of their lives, it makes you understand just what they are capable of within your class. Plus, the students are much more willing to accept those expectations as a result of the support you've shown them."

Coach Kennedy also understands that in order to get the most *from* his students, he has to first invest *in* his students. "I have seen this pay off by having students work hard for me on and off the field because of the fact that I recognized them in areas outside of my soccer program. Whether it's seeing them on stage, in another classroom, or at a different sporting event, I want my students to know that I care about them as people." He says showing care and respect for students means that he can raise the bar when it comes to expectations.

Many of today's classroom management issues may be a result of the students not connecting with their teachers. Attending various events and activities at your school is a great way to strengthen these student/teacher relationships. If your students know that you care about them *outside* of the classroom, they will be more willing to show you that they care about their work *inside* the classroom.

Gary Gaines, the head football coach featured in the movie *Friday Night Lights*, understood the importance of making these connections with his players. He knew that in order to get the most out of his players on the field, he first needed to understand who they were off the field. Day in and day out, Coach Gaines's players saw him sharing his time with them, and in return, they gave him their best effort. And while he understood the importance of winning, he focused even more on relationships. "Being perfect is not about that scoreboard out there. It's not about winning. It's about you and your relationship with yourself, your family, and your friends. Being perfect is about being able to look your friends in the eye and know that you didn't let them down because you told them the truth. And that truth is you did everything you could. There wasn't one more thing you could've done," he said to his players.

Imagine showing that kind of allegiance to your students! Supporting your students at their events is a meaningful and effective way to show them that you care. And while it will take more of your time and energy to make this happen, it's important to remember that we ask a great deal from our students each day in our classes, and we should be willing to give a little back in return. Simply put, being a movie teacher requires more than just teaching your class. It means giving "everything you can" to your students.

GET 'EM UP AND
GET 'EM MOVING!

The Importance of Controlled
Movement In the Classroom

HACK 4

A desk is a dangerous place from which to view the world.
– JOHN LE CARRÉ, AUTHOR

THE PROBLEM: STUDENTS SIT WAY TOO MUCH

THINK FOR A minute about what your students' day at school looks like. For the sake of this example, let's say the school day starts when they get on the bus at 7:30 a.m. and ends when they finish their homework (which of course they do immediately after school) at 4:30 p.m. All told, that's nine hours of school per day.

Now, think about how much of that day they spend sitting. Students sit on the bus, in their morning classes, at the lunch table, and then finish off the day at school parked in the desks of their afternoon classes. Once they leave school, more sitting takes place as they grab a seat on the bus ride home, followed by an additional thirty to sixty minutes of sitting as they complete their homework. And this doesn't even include any sitting that might happen during assemblies or special meetings that might pop up during the school day! With all that sitting going on, is it any wonder that your students get a little squirrely during class?

THE HACK: GET 'EM UP AND GET 'EM MOVING!

Letting your students get up and move in a controlled manner during class is crucial to effective classroom management. By simply allowing students to move periodically, you will reduce the number of disruptive situations, thus improving the overall classroom experience for everyone. As a general rule, I have always tried to implement a ten-minute rule in my class. The logic behind this idea is that no lesson where I am explicitly teaching a concept should last longer than ten minutes. That seems to be the length of time students can successfully sit and listen before their interest starts to stray. And while this isn't necessarily true in all situations, as far as direct instruction in a classroom environment goes, ten minutes seems to be about the limit.

You may be thinking, *But how will adding more movement improve classroom management?* While I know this might sound contradictory, allowing your students to move about the classroom in a controlled manner will greatly improve class behavior. Often, students who go to the bathroom or who get up to sharpen their pencils are doing so simply because they are bored or just need to get the wiggles out. And once they get up, they often take a roundabout manner to get to their destination, disrupting their fellow students and the overall flow of the class in the process.

 Movement gets students excited about the activity itself, and also gets them actively involved in the learning.

This is why it's so important to control the movement in your class. And no, this does not mean that students aren't allowed to leave their seats. In fact, it's quite the opposite. Controlled movement occurs when students are moving based around the learning. By creating these types of opportunities, you, as the teacher, get to guide when and how this movement happens. So rather than disrupting the class through random movements like sharpening pencils or going to the bathroom, students will actually be engaged in the learning environment through their actions.

There are numerous ways to effectively initiate controlled movement within the classroom, each with its own benefits and time requirements.

Write it on the board. Rather than you writing on the board when your students share ideas or answers, allow your students the chance to go to the board and write down their thoughts. This gets them moving, and it allows them to have a more authentic engagement with the learning. This is quick and easy, and can usually be done in less than thirty seconds per student. But make sure to stagger which kids go to the board. Sending thirty students at once to write on the board creates a serious logjam, and I can tell you from experience that nothing good has ever happened *in the history of teaching* when thirty students with nothing to do get crammed together within a three-foot radius.

Turn-n-talk. After presenting a concept to the class, have students turn-n-talk with one another about what they just learned. The simple act of turning around creates enough movement that students may not feel the need to get up later. This is another fast activity, and I recommend spending one minute or less in these discussions as a way to keep everyone actively engaged from start to finish.

Musical chairs. If you're looking to have an active discussion with multiple questions, have your students change seats each time you present them with a new question. If you really want to get creative, put on music while they change seats and have them sit once the music ends. Here's how it looks: Have all your students stand up next to their desks. Let them know that they can move around only while the music is playing. Once the music stops, they need to sit in the closest empty chair. This arrangement then becomes a discussion group for the question. Once that question is over, they stand up and repeat the process.

You will be amazed at how engaged they will be if you play five or ten seconds of their favorite songs. (I recommend not going longer than that. When they're given too much time to complete a simple task, classroom management begins to fall apart.) And if you really want to mess with your students, learn the lyrics of some of these songs and sing along! I often use the free iTunes samples as a way to vary the songs that I play. The length of time for this activity depends on how many questions you have and how long you want to dedicate to each song.

Walk-n-talk. This one takes a lesson on the road! Rather than sitting in class presenting your lesson, pair students up and go walk around the neighborhood, school campus, or field discussing the topic. Here's an example:

1. Figure out where you want to hold your walk-n-talk. My class usually goes around our local neighborhood, but playing fields and tracks are also great for this activity.

2. Have students pair up and stand side-by-side in two parallel lines. Each group should be separated by about two feet.

3. Ask the first question, then have the group slowly start walking as they discuss the topic. As they walk, you are walking up and down the line, listening to the conversations to make sure students are touching on essential information.

4. After one or two minutes (depending on the depth of the question), have the students wrap up their comments. Again, for the sake of classroom management, it's better to have students exit each question a few seconds too early than to let them go one second too long. As an added bonus, the question is officially ended once the students have thanked their partners and shaken hands. I always end each question this way so students can actively engage in the positive standards I expect from them.

5. Before asking the next question, have the students in the left line move one position forward (with the front going to the back). Students then greet their new partners (again with a handshake), followed by you providing the next question.

6. Repeat until you have covered the topic.

Like musical chairs, the timing of this one depends on the number of questions. From my experience, a solid walk-n-talk will take twenty to thirty minutes to fully implement (leave class, walk, return to class). And while that is a great deal of time, it will be well worth it once you see the increased level of engagement.

Standing desks. If you are really looking to shake things up, consider investing in some standing desks. Many of the newer standing desks designed for students come complete with a rocker-bar at the bottom that allows students to quietly shake, rattle, and roll without disrupting the rest of the class. These desks keep the students at eye level, which in itself helps to keep the class engaged in the learning. Desks like these are especially beneficial for those students who, no matter how hard they try, just can't keep themselves from moving. (See Act 4: Standing Desks.)

Behind the Scenes Act 4: Standing Desks

There are many ways to gauge whether a lesson is successful, but one of the biggest indicators for me is when my students start to question when we are going to do a certain activity again. There is no sweeter sound than a student asking, "Can we do a walk-n-talk today?" or saying, "When can we do that musical chairs thing again?" Movement gets students excited about the activity itself, and also gets them actively involved in the learning.

WHAT YOU CAN DO TOMORROW

While you might not be ready to go all-in on this idea quite yet, here are some ideas to help get the ball rolling.

- **TRY A TURN-N-TALK. As described above, implement a turn-n-talk discussion** as the easiest possible way to introduce movement to your class. This is a great activity because it requires no pre-planning (beyond the discussion questions you were going to ask anyway) or seat rearrangement.

- **HAVE STUDENTS ACT OUT THE LEARNING.** Acting out a scene from a book or a key concept from a lesson is a great way to excite students about the learning. As any teacher can tell you, students love drama, and this hack gives them an opportunity to put it to productive use.

  - Need to review vocabulary terms for a test? What about pairing students up and letting them act out the words to one another.

  - Want to do an informal assessment? Divide the class in half, and have students play charades using the key concepts presented.

  - Looking to do a unit review? In groups of four, let students create a two-minute movie that summarizes all the essential information from the unit.

- **PLAN A WALKING ROUTE.** Explore the areas in and around your school to see what options are available for a walk-n-talk. I suggest finding two routes. One for shorter discussions (ten minutes or less) and one for longer discussions (more than ten minutes).

- **RESEARCH STANDING DESKS.** There is an abundance of information out there touting the physical and mental benefits of using a standing desk. Take a few minutes and see what the research says. If you agree with it, spend a few more minutes investigating the various brands and prices to see if some might fit into your school's furniture budget for next year.

A BLUEPRINT FOR FULL IMPLEMENTATION

Step 1: Decide to get moving.

Before anything else can happen, be willing to make the choice that you are going to actively try this out. Controlled movement should be included in your daily lessons, even multiple times per day, so it is imperative that you believe in what you're doing.

Step 2: Find some spots where movement fits within your current curriculum.

Like all else related to teaching, implementing controlled movement into your class will take a little planning. Look over your upcoming lessons and see if there are spots where you could include some of the suggested movements into your day. Teachers are often surprised at how easily movement can be added to what they already do, and many of the ideas can be adapted to fit pretty much any topic. So while there is no need to redo all your lessons to make this work, it does require you to reevaluate how your students engage themselves with the learning.

Step 3: Get moving!

This is the moment when you incorporate movement into part of your lesson. When introducing this concept to your class, make sure you are clear about both the guidelines of the assignment and the parameters of the movement. But be warned—activities like these often get a little loud. That said, it's also important to keep in mind that learning doesn't have to be a quiet activity.

Step 4: Start finding new ways to move.

Once you have incorporated controlled movement into your established lessons, start looking for ways to include it into your new lessons as you create them. Rather than it being an additional activity you throw in, make lessons involving movement that are intentional and purposeful for the learning.

Step 5: Arrange your class to allow for more movement.

After establishing movement as part of your regular routine, try organizing your room in a way that invites students to get up and move. Using a variety of seating arrangements for the different activities will not only accommodate the movement, it will also create an element of anticipation for students as they walk in the door and see a new classroom layout.

Step 6: Purchase some standing desks.

Standing desks allow your students to move on a daily basis, even when the lesson doesn't specifically call for it. These desks are great classroom management resources in that students who stand are able to shake out their jitters without disrupting the overall flow of the class. Plus, from my experience, standing up helps students stay focused and connected to what is happening, and that engagement further limits the chances of students interrupting the learning. And while I'm not a fan of seating charts (see Hack 1), you may need a system for rotating students so that everyone gets a chance to use the desks. Take the opportunity to discuss a fair plan with your students.

OVERCOMING PUSHBACK

Incorporating controlled movement into your class may be a scary concept, especially when it's often the uncontrolled movements that cause so many classroom management issues. Here are some common concerns related to implementing this hack.

This won't work with my class. If I let them get up they'll get out of control. While every class is different, the vast majority would benefit from incorporating more movement into the daily routine, especially with clear instructions and boundaries. The key is that these controlled movement sessions are well planned and structured. Besides the specific learning targets you are trying to reach, you should also include time limits to each activity. Simply put, cutting a discussion fifteen seconds short is more beneficial for class management than having it run fifteen seconds over. If you're a teacher, you know what I'm talking about! It's almost scary to see how much havoc a bored student can unleash in fifteen seconds!

But won't some of these activities be loud? In a word—yes. But here's the thing: Learning isn't supposed to be a spectator sport, and when students are actively involved in what is happening, there's bound to be some noise! But it's productive noise. I even argue that the most engaging classes are generally the loudest ones. In fact, it's the quiet rooms, where you only hear the teacher talking, that freak me out! Besides, are you really going to get mad at a student who is talking too loudly *about the topic at hand*? I would hope not!

My school doesn't have the budget for standing desks. Teachers often think their schools don't have any money for optional items like this, but they never follow through to find out for sure. Schools and districts generally have a furniture budget every year to replace needed items like desks and chairs. If this is part of the plan, taking the extra steps to research the cost of standing desks could be extremely beneficial. Rather than spending a certain amount on the same replacement desks and chairs, see if that money could instead be spent on new standing desks for your classroom. And while it's true that some standing desks are rather pricy, there are basic models that can have the same positive benefits (without all the flash) at a price that is competitive to a traditional desk and chair.

Also keep in mind that you don't need to do a complete overhaul and change out all of the traditional desks at once. I started out with only four standing desks that first year. I quickly discovered that students *loved* using them, and before every period, they would race into my class to get one of them. Because of that initial success, I added another six the following year. And ten more the year after that. My new classroom goal is to be completely sitting-desk-free (but with a few stashed in the corner for emergencies) within the next two years.

Finally, if there truly isn't any money in the budget for this, there are still ways to make this happen. Cities and states often have grants for teachers, and crowdfunding sites like donorschoose.org and gofundme.com can serve as valuable resources in your quest for cash. And while all of these will require effort on your part, the benefits are definitely worth it.

THE HACK IN ACTION

Campbell Ainsworth, a middle school Spanish teacher, is a big believer in using movement as a way to limit classroom management issues. "Working as a language teacher and with middle school students, incorporating movement into the daily routine is important. I believe it helps them retain the information better, and that being active while engaging with the material is a way to help students maintain their energy and focus for the entire class period."

Ainsworth mixes up his groups while discussing a concept or working at stations. He has found that this allows students the opportunity to work with different peers at different levels. Also, the consistent movement helps keep students on task, and for students who are easily distracted (or are themselves distracting), it limits having to work with the same partner for a long period of time.

"I use a lot of drama, too. When I introduce vocabulary, we move all the desks to the side and students have to get in partners and act out the words as they repeat them. The actions and movement help them internalize the difficult vocabulary, and it also lowers their inhibitions to speak as they have to focus on the movement/drama task," he says. Ainsworth adds that the movement doesn't have to last long, and that including even a little movement has benefits. "Movement makes any activity dynamic and gives a sense of urgency to the task." He is considering a no-desk classroom next year in order to give kids more space for movement and to use manipulatives.

In *Dead Poets Society*, English teacher John Keating utilized the idea of controlled movement as a way to enhance the learning and to solidify his relationships with his students. Whether he was teaching a lesson on conformity as students march around the courtyard, having students recite famous quotes while kicking a soccer ball on the field, or letting his students stand on their desks to get a different perspective of the world, Mr. Keating took every opportunity to incorporate movement into his curriculum. And while others often frowned upon his methods, he believed that in order to fully engage his students, he, along with all teachers, must constantly look at things in a different way. Rather than sticking to the status quo of teaching, he opted to do what he knew was in the best interest of his students.

For years, students have been told to "Sit still and listen," and frankly, it's time for a more effective and modern teaching style. Controlled movement has changed how I manage my class, as well as the learning that occurs within it. Moving in this manner allows students to involve both their bodies and their minds in the learning process, and as result, the students are more engaged and receptive to learning. As an added bonus, the constant interruptions of students getting up and disrupting the class flow have been eliminated. I'm confident that, if you give it a shot, the same will happen within your class.

WALK THEIR WALK AND TALK THEIR TALK

Using Social Media as a Learning Tool

HACK 5

*You can either allow social media to be helpful for you
or it can be harmful. I like to let it be helpful.*
— CIARA, MUSICIAN

THE PROBLEM: SCHOOLS FAIL TO UTILIZE SOCIAL MEDIA

SOCIAL MEDIA IS everywhere. For many of today's students, it has been a part of their lives for as long as they have been alive. It's how they communicate, plan, and maintain their lives. But here's what I don't get: Why are schools so against using this to their advantage?

One of the major factors causing students to misbehave is the simple fact that they are disengaged from the learning. This can be the result of the topic being boring to the subject being too easy or too difficult. But regardless of the cause, if your class isn't into what they are doing, it becomes difficult to maintain control of the room. And this is where social media comes in.

In today's classrooms, there are so many different learning styles and abilities within a single class that, even with an array of differentiated strategies, it's challenging to get all the students engaged at the same time. But social media is the great equalizer amongst today's students, and when teachers use it to their advantage, the class instantly becomes offensive minded (actively learning) rather than defensive minded (disrupting the learning). Getting everyone involved and excited about learning is what separates a movie-type teacher from the rest, and using social media in the classroom is a great way to accomplish this.

THE HACK: WALK THEIR WALK AND TALK THEIR TALK

Here's a little secret: If your class is *fully* engaged in what they are doing, classroom management takes care of itself. When these moments happen, it's like the ultimate movie-teacher moment. Time seems to fly by, all of your students are working to their highest abilities, and just when you're sure that your students are going to go all *Dead Poets Society* on you and stand on their desks and cry out, "O Captain, My Captain" … a student gets bored with what he is doing, so he asks to go to the bathroom. And just like that, reality rears its ugly head. This is where social media comes to the rescue. Assignments geared around social media will keep your students engaged, and there may actually be times when you have to ask them to *stop* working on their assignments. That's how into these assignments they will get!

Letting your students teach you shows that you are a learner just like them, and this will further strengthen your relationships with your students.

Because of their popularity, social media outlets like YouTube, Twitter, and Instagram have already set up a formula for success within the classroom. And because your students already understand how they work, all you have to do is be willing to adapt some of your ideas to fit the mold. The coolest part of this hack is that you can successfully implement it in two different ways. If your school allows you and your students to access social media, then you can use channels such as Twitter and Instagram in their direct forms. On the other hand, if your school limits or blocks the use of social media, the ideas presented here can just as easily be implemented using the old-school pen-and-paper method. Here are some examples:

YouTube. No matter what you're teaching, there is a YouTube video that could be used to enhance the learning of that topic. And don't take the easy route on these. Find a music video or a basketball highlight film to supplement the ideas you are discussing in class. These videos can serve a range of purposes. Whether they are used as writing prompts for a starter activity, shown mid-class to introduce a new concept, or at the end of the period to solidify a point, there are multiple ways to incorporate YouTube videos into any curriculum. My one suggestion is to use videos that are less than five minutes. Remember, these should be used to support the topic, not be the focus of it.

Twitter. I call this idea "two hundred and eighty characters of brilliance!" I will often ask students to create a tweet that summarizes the learning for the day. This is a great opportunity for students to work collaboratively with one another. Plus, students love using emojis and hashtags with this, so it really allows them the chance to write creatively. This is also a great way to teach clear and concise writing. Doing these with a pen and paper can also serve as a quick and easy exit ticket activity. (See Act 5: Sample Tweet.)

Twitter Summary - Sample Tweet

SAMPLE
@sample

Lord of the Flies - Chapter II

OMG! I can't believe Roger killed Piggy! And what's up w/ the savages? Don't they want 2 b rescued? #idiots #watch4fallingrocks

Behind the Scenes Act 5: Sample Tweet

Finally, I have learned over time that students *really* love to share these, so make sure you leave some time for them to present their tweets. And while this might seem like a simple assignment, it encompasses a wide range of skills including collaboration, summarization, concise writing, creativity, and public speaking.

Instagram. This is similar to the Twitter idea, only this one includes pictures (either taken on a phone or hand-drawn) to support the caption. Students take pride in doing these, so don't hesitate to hang these up in your room or the hallway. You will be amazed at how something as simple as displaying student work can positively impact the classroom environment. And if you have visual learners, let them summarize an assignment in this visual way to differentiate the learning.

But be warned, the Instagram assignment takes longer to complete, so this is usually done in class or as homework. Depending on what they are summarizing, students can take/draw anywhere from one to four pictures that reflect the main ideas presented (either in class or from the reading). And when you consider that each of those pictures comes with a caption, it's clear to see how this assignment could easily eat up an hour or more. Because of this, I recommend setting limits on how long they can work on these. While it's great that they are so engaged with the assignment, you still want to make sure they are managing their time efficiently (and keeping up on their work in other classes).

Rather than fighting against social media, this hack encourages you to use it to your advantage. (For even more ideas on using social media in the classroom, check out the EdTech Missions in *Hacking Digital Learning Strategies* by Shelly Sanchez Terrell). Engagement is a key element to making a lasting impression on your class, and in today's world, social media is an engagement magnet. But keep this in mind: Don't ruin something fun and interactive like social media by making it all serious and school-like. You can still have a learning target for the assignment; just make sure it can be reached in a creative and engaging manner.

WHAT YOU CAN DO TOMORROW

Whether you are new to this whole social media thing or a savvy veteran, here are some simple ideas to liven up your teaching.

- **TALK TO YOUR STUDENTS ABOUT WHAT KINDS OF SOCIAL MEDIA THEY USE.** As students walk into your class tomorrow, do an informal survey where you ask them what types of social media platforms they use. If you're looking for more formal data, take a quick poll in class regarding the various options.

- **FAMILIARIZE YOURSELF WITH THE DIFFERENT OUTLETS.** Spend some time getting to know the pros and cons of each social media outlet. Cyberspace changes quickly, and what was once popular (AOL, MySpace) can disappear in an instant. To get the most out of this hack, make sure you are incorporating platforms that your students already use and enjoy.

- **LEARN THE LANGUAGE.** Tweets, hashtags, tagging, emojis, memes, and GIFs are terms that your students know. You will want to brush up on these, and other terms, as a way to talk-the-talk with your students. A quick search of "social media terms" should get you up to speed.

- **WATCH A FUNNY YOUTUBE VIDEO.** While there are probably hundreds of videos out there about the *subject* you are teaching, to connect with your students, start class by showing a funny video that supports the *concept* you are studying. This is sure to grab their attention, and it sets a great tone for the rest of the period.

- **TRY TWEETING.** For the bold who want to dive right in, have your students create a Twitter summary (written or digital) that summarizes the learning that took place in your class. To make it even more engaging, ask them to include at least one hashtag at the end. And if your school allows it and you're feeling extra adventurous, ask them to tag someone in their tweets.

- **ASSIGN AN INSTAGRAM SUMMARY.** When presenting a concept to your class tomorrow, have students take notes without using words. I suggest keeping this short (less than five minutes), but then giving students the chance to share and explain their artwork or photos.

A BLUEPRINT FOR FULL IMPLEMENTATION

Step 1: Set up your accounts.

The best way to get to know social media is to play around with it. If you don't have a Twitter or Instagram account, I suggest setting them up. And when considering your Twitter handle, it's wise to go with a name that's easy, catchy, and short. Mine is @baldroberts.

Step 2: Find out how it works.

Once your accounts are set up, send out a tweet or post, and start following people! In addition to helping you better understand how to utilize this resource in class, it can serve as a valuable teaching tool as you begin to follow other teachers and professional organizations from around the world. Odds are your favorite teacher, author, and educational consultant all have accounts, and now you will have access to everything they have to offer.

Step 3: Create a social-media-related assignment.

Each of the three examples mentioned earlier (YouTube, Twitter, Instagram) can serve as simple, yet effective, starters or exit tickets. At the same time, they can also be expanded if you are looking for something with a little more meat to it. Don't hesitate to ask your students for ideas regarding how to incorporate more social media into your curriculum.

Step 4: Let students share their work.

Students love sharing assignments like these, so make sure you leave time for them to present their work. At the end of class, I often let my students vote on the best tweet, and I have been known to hang up Instagram pictures on my classroom walls. Students will work hard to impress their peers with these!

Step 5: Keep looking for new social media connections.

As previously mentioned, social media is constantly changing. That means if you keep up to date, more and more of these opportunities will become available each year. Plus, if you ask, I am sure your students will be more than willing to share their thoughts on how to incorporate channels like Snapchat into their learning.

OVERCOMING PUSHBACK

The use of social media in schools is a pretty divisive issue. Here are some common concerns that may arise when implementing this hack.

My school blocks social media. The Twitter and Instagram examples presented here are only *based* on social media, and do not actually require *using* social media. If you are able to use the full platform within your school, do it! But if not, written examples are just as effective. As for the YouTube videos, you can download and save those at home, then play the files when at school.

I'm not comfortable using social media. That's OK. You can still implement the pen-and-paper versions of these activities, and your students will still be engaged because they are super comfortable using social media concepts. That's one of the best parts about this. If you have any questions about how it works, you have a room full of experts ready to help. Letting your students teach you shows that you are a learner just like them, and this will further strengthen your relationships with your students.

I don't need to use social media to teach the skills I want students to learn. You are probably right on this one. But let me ask you this: Are you looking to teach the skills, or do you want your students to *learn* the skills? From my experience, getting them to learn is much easier if they are engaged with the way the skill is being presented, and social media does just that.

THE HACK IN ACTION

Carrie Barney, a fourth-grade teacher, knew a bit about Twitter and how it worked when she decided to utilize the Twitter summary with her class. The first time they tried it, they were discussing an article they'd read earlier in the week. And then something beautiful happened: The Twitter-savvy students filled in the gaps for their peers by explaining what they knew about Tweets. This gave her class the buy-in that was needed to try something new, and as this was happening, anticipation to try it started to build. "When I let them know that they could use emojis, well, that was it!" she said. A few minutes later, after setting up the guidelines, expectations, and modeling the assignment, she set them loose.

"All of my students were writing. Every. Single. One. Total engagement!" she explains. "That right there is the dream. The dream!" And this success has continued in Mrs. Barney's room ever since. She says she's tried the Twitter summary across various subjects and has seen the same level of engagement. Additionally, she noticed that the more they worked on their Tweets, the less she had to manage the behavior of the class.

In watching this unfold, the positive impact that social media can have on a classroom environment became clear to her, and she was excited to share her new success story with her peers. "At our school's next faculty meeting, when it was time for sharing celebrations, I had to share mine. The following week, next thing I know, I was being pulled into my colleagues' classes and shown *their* Twitter walls." From her experience, using social media as a way to productively engage her students has resulted in overwhelming success. The scariest part—"Just being brave enough to try it out!"—wasn't so bad after all.

In *Mr. Holland's Opus*, music teacher Glenn Holland understood the importance that relevancy can have on the success of a lesson. "Playing music is supposed to be fun. It's about heart, it's about feelings," he said. Unfortunately, his message was being lost as a result of his students not connecting with the classical music that they were studying. So as any great teacher would do, Mr. Holland decided to adapt his teaching methods to better fit the needs of his students by meshing the classical music that he loved with some of the contemporary songs that his students enjoyed. When he did this, his students' hands were up in the air, they were answering questions, and it looked like fun.

Mr. Holland realized that in order to have music impact his students in a meaningful manner, he needed to make it resonate with them in a way that went beyond simply learning the notes. He wanted them to understand and *feel* what making music was like, and he was better able to accomplish this once he was willing to use all the tools at his disposal, including contemporary music.

Social media is like the contemporary music in this film: It's a modern tool that engages students in the learning. The best part about this hack is that you can still implement the learning targets into the lesson, but those objectives won't become the *focus* of the lesson. The learning is still taking place, but it's just more secretive in how it happens. So rather than constantly fighting against what students enjoy, I encourage you to change your mindset and embrace social media as the valuable classroom resource that it is.

LET'S GET PERSONAL

Creating Opportunities for
Personalized Learning

HACK 6

Today you are You, that is truer than true.
There is no one alive who is Youer than You.
– DR. SEUSS, AUTHOR

THE PROBLEM: TEACHERS TEACH THEIR
CONTENT RATHER THAN THEIR STUDENTS

THE LECTURE. It's been a part of teaching for as long as teaching itself. And while its effectiveness has come under scrutiny over the past few years, there are numerous reasons why it has been able to survive throughout time, including:

- Teachers control the ideas being presented.

- A great deal of information can be shared quickly.

- The topic can be presented to a very large audience.

- It provides a very low-risk environment for students.

And while it might not be the most popular opinion, I honestly believe that lecturing has a place within the context of today's classroom. Not exactly what you expect to hear from a book about becoming a movie-type teacher, eh?

Well, you're right. While I do think lecturing can be an effective teaching method, I also don't feel that it should be the *only* teaching method. And too often, as a result of overcrowded classes, the need to cover the required curriculum, or just a fear of releasing some of their power, teachers fall back on this tried-and-tested method. As a result, teachers often end up teaching the *content* rather than teaching the *students*.

 To personalize learning, adjust your teaching to fit your students' learning styles rather than having them adjust to your teaching style.

So what's the difference, you ask? Teaching the *content* is a passive learning environment. Engagement is minimal, opportunities to ask questions are limited, and students take in and think about the information individually. Teaching *students,* in contrast, creates an active learning environment. Engagement is high, questions are frequently asked, and students are working with one another and sharing their ideas as they learn.

One of my former college students said it best when he explained that the difference between teaching content and teaching students is similar to the difference between watching a movie and playing a video game. Movies, he said, provide the viewer with everything they need. All that is required is showing up and sitting back in your chair (and possibly falling asleep). Video games, on the other hand, require planning, thought, and teamwork. It's an exciting experience where the players take chances, overcome obstacles, and reap the rewards of their hard work.

So using the above analogy, if you were to ask your students to categorize your class, would they say it's a movie or a video game?

THE HACK: LET'S GET PERSONAL

Take a second and think about your favorite book, movie, and song. Now spend another few seconds thinking about what you love about that particular book, movie, and song.

If you're like me, you connect with your favorites because of some personal reason. In *To Kill a Mockingbird*, I relate with Atticus Finch and his belief that people should stay true to their values regardless of the situation. In *Good Will Hunting*, it's the unbreakable loyalty that the characters played by Matt Damon and Ben Affleck have toward one another that really impacts me. And as far as *A Boy Named Sue* goes, it's the simple rhythm and narrative of the song that makes me love it so much.

Now think about this: What if I took away your favorites and told you that you could only enjoy my favorites because I think mine are better? I'm betting that a few of you would love my choices and would be perfectly fine with that. I am also guessing that some of you would be indifferent to my selections. Finally, it's safe to say that a bunch of you would just plain hate my picks, and as a result, would dread every time you had to read, watch, or listen to one of my selections.

Here's how this all relates to this hack: Teachers often teach the way that is best for them (my favorites) rather than focusing on the methods that are best for the individual student (your favorites). To truly become a movie-type teacher, it's important to realize that a teacher's job is not to present information to the class, but rather to make sure that the students *learn* what is being taught. Providing students with a more personalized approach does this.

This hack centers on creating more personalized learning opportunities for your students. Doing so will positively impact the learning atmosphere of your class by allowing students to work in ways that best fit their skill levels, but also the learning styles that work well for them. And while trying to personalize learning for every student may sound daunting, it can be accomplished with only a few minor tweaks to what many teachers currently do.

There are numerous ways to improve student learning and engagement, and some may require you to adjust the standards based on your class and community. But whether it's through how you teach, the way you group students, or your assessments, here are some strategies to help you personalize the learning.

Vary your teaching method. To truly personalize learning, make an effort to reach every student by varying how you present information. While the lecture format mentioned earlier might be effective for some students (thus showing that it still deserves a place in class), I feel confident in saying that it isn't the best approach for *all* students. To help with this, try using a wide range of instructional strategies throughout the day.

Simple yet effective alternatives to lecturing include showing relevant and engaging video clips to supplement a discussion, listening to a podcast to reinforce a concept, or playing a review game to summarize the main ideas from a unit. And remember, this should happen on a daily basis, not just when it's convenient for you. Simply put: To personalize learning, adjust your teaching to fit your students' learning styles rather than having them adjust to your teaching style.

Let students self-select their groups. While you should still establish the parameters of the groups (i.e., no more than four per group), give your students the opportunity to figure out who they work best with. To mix things up, request that they not repeat partners from one project to the next, which makes them branch out from their friends. This includes the option of letting students work by themselves if they so choose. Your students know themselves pretty well, and sometimes they may need a little break from their friends. One of the biggest causes of classroom disruptions stems from students being frustrated by what is happening in class, and working in groups can often trigger this frustration. If you can decrease this stress by allowing students to work with people they are comfortable with, the result will be a more productive use of class time for everyone involved (including you).

Allow for student choice on assignments and tests. Instead of having one option for an assignment or a test, provide students with a variety of options where they can show their understanding of the subject. The end goal is that your students reach the learning target set for them, and the best way to help them accomplish this is to allow them to connect their learning to something that is of interest and meaningful to them. Possible options for this are:

1. **Provide students with a variety of options as a way for them to showcase their learning.** Instead of a traditional final exam, I often provide a written option (i.e., writing a paper about the learning), an artistic option (i.e., drawing a visual representation of the learning), or a technological option (i.e., making a movie about the learning). Providing students with a range of choices gives them the chance to express what they learned in a way that offers them a voice in the process. This simple act will help students become more engaged in

the learning, thus creating fewer opportunities for classroom distractions. (See Act 6: Final Project Options.)

To Kill a Mockingbird

The Assignment –

For your final project, please select one of the options from the list below.

The Requirements –

The learning target for this assignment is to effectively use textual evidence as support for your ideas, so please make sure that your project provides at least three examples of evidence from the novel. Also, don't forget to include a works cited page.

PROJECT OPTIONS –

Option One: Type a two-page paper that describes the character from the novel who changes the most throughout the story. Please have at least one quote per body paragraph.

Option Two: Analyze a contemporary song and relate the themes of the song to the novel. Be sure to include specific lines from both the song and the book.

Option Three: Build a miniature version of Maycomb based on the descriptions given in the book. This can be created by hand (popsicle sticks, Legos) or on a computer (Minecraft). Either way, a map key must be provided for the various houses and objects.

Option Four: Create a video where you act out Chapter 32 from the novel. Be sure to include a written transcript that incorporates quotes from earlier in the story.

Option Five: Draw a graphic novel version of the story. You must include 15-20 frames, and at least a third of the pictures must contain words.

Final Thoughts –

If you choose to collaborate with a partner or in a group, you can select who you want to work with. But remember, work with people who will push you up, not pull you down!

Behind the Scenes Act 6: Final Project Options

2. **Give students a list of formative assessment choices and a required point total.** This is a portfolio-based assessment where students create and turn in assignments that add up to a certain number of points. Students who want to challenge themselves can choose the most complex option, thus fulfilling the requirements of the assignment all at once. Meanwhile, students who prefer a buffet-style of assessments can still demonstrate what they learned by completing two or three less-complicated projects, thus also satisfying the point requirements. This allows students to personally select the assessment methods that work best for them. Plus, if you make all the options engaging and fun, you will be amazed at how many students submit *more* than the required number of points!

3. **Let students have total control over an assessment.** For the *really* brave, a third option is to give your students complete control over their final assessment. I call this one the "Do Something That Impresses Me" option. Simply put, after we have completed a unit, I ask students to create a project that not only shows me what they have learned, but also impresses me. After nearly twenty years of teaching, my students know that I am difficult to impress, and it is fun to see them push themselves. Additionally, they also complete a self-assessment explaining how their project reaches the learning target and why I should be impressed by it (see Hack 7). Some of my favorites

include a student learning how to unicycle specifically for this project, another who taught the class how to ride a horse *while riding a horse* on the back field of the school, and a third who built an automatic watering system for the class plants. Needless to say, I was impressed by all of those!

By creating more opportunities for personalized learning, your students will actually be excited to complete the work, and with this excitement will come a more active and productive level of student involvement. The end result of this is increased engagement and learning, and decreased boredom and problematic behavior.

WHAT YOU CAN DO TOMORROW

Personalized learning is a term that strikes fear in the hearts of many teachers. And I don't blame them. With so many different types of learners and abilities in a class, it can feel overwhelming to think about trying to connect with each of them individually. But that's what movie teachers do! Here are a few ideas to help get you started.

- **DO A PRE-ASSESSMENT.** When I first began teaching, I assumed I knew my students' level regarding the topic at hand, and I started each unit at that level. And while I usually did a decent job in my estimation, there were always a few students who were either already ahead of where I began or who were way behind the starting point.

Pre-assessments allow students to show you what, if any, prior knowledge they are bringing to the table. This will give you an opportunity to personalize the lessons as a way to fully engage all of your students.

• Two of the primary causes of classroom misbehavior are boredom (when students already know the information presented) and lack of understanding (when the information is way too complicated), and doing a pre-assessment helps to decrease the chances of both of these from happening. Three of my favorite pre-assessment strategies are asking my students to give real-world examples of key words related to the topic, having them complete a KWL (Know, Wonder, Learned), and rating their initial understanding (on a scale of 1-5) from a list of unit-related topics.

• **INVESTIGATE ALTERNATIVE WAYS TO PRESENT THE INFORMATION.** While I know it is more comfortable to stick with the same old methods that you've used for years, the purpose of this hack is to inspire you to update a few of those methods. Making the learning more personalized doesn't mean creating an entirely new curriculum; it just means that you can add a few more options to your teaching menu. So take a few minutes to look over what you currently do, and ask yourself if there are any spots where you might be able to add in a few more personalized choices for your students.

- **PILOT LETTING STUDENTS SELF-SELECT THEIR GROUPS.** If you're not quite ready to let students select their own project partners, ease into it by letting them work on an informal assignment together. This is a safe way to explore if you want to do this in the future without dedicating much time and energy to the process. As your students work, keep an eye the situation and take note of what is or isn't working. The first time I try a new activity, I always let them know that this is a pilot, and the results will determine if I am going to continue it in the future. This usually helps my students put forth their best efforts, and they always let me know which ideas are keepers. Hopefully, as a result of letting students select their groups, you will see students who are excited and engaged with their groups and with the learning itself.

A BLUEPRINT FOR FULL IMPLEMENTATION

Step 1: Reflect on the various teaching methods you currently use.

Spend a few minutes and write down all the ways that you share information with your class, as well as how you assess the learning. Make sure you have specific examples demonstrating each method. Once you have a list, reflect on the effectiveness of each method and assessment. If you are struggling to come up with specifics, try recording yourself for a class period or two. As you review the video, pay attention to how much time you spend on the various teaching and assessment methods that you implement during each class. Things you will want to pay attention to include how much talking you do versus how much your students do, the frequency with which you break students into groups, how often you provide your students with opportunities to learn via outside sources (pictures, music, videos), and the ways you formatively assess student learning. Finally, if by chance you are hesitant to record yourself, asking a colleague to observe and discuss what your teaching looks like from their perspective also serves this purpose well.

Step 2: Look for places to personalize learning.

Once you have created a list of your teaching methods, focus your attention on trying to personalize those methods for your students. Instead of requiring notes from every student, give them the option of summarizing the lecture in a paragraph or a picture. Or, instead of only providing one example about a topic, you could open it up to your students and see what kinds of connections they can build around the topic. Think about what is causing the method you're using to be ineffective. Then brainstorm ideas around how you might improve things by adding more student choice to the learning process.

Step 3: Add variety and choice.

Look for ways to vary how you present information, as well as letting students self-select assignments of interest. And don't forget that open-ended assignments (completely selected by the student) serve as a great way to let them drive their learning!

Step 4: Consistently reflect on the process.

As the unit progresses, take time to reflect on what is or is not working. This can be as simple as writing a plus (+) or a minus (-) next to the lesson or method in your planner. Also, allow students to share their thoughts on the situation. Remember, while it might not be the most comfortable method for you, if it works for your students, you'll want to take that into serious consideration.

OVERCOMING PUSHBACK

Change is hard, and I fully understand why you might have concerns about incorporating this hack into your classroom. To help ease this fear, here are some thoughts on common concerns regarding personalized learning.

What about the students who don't have friends to join during group projects? This is always a tough one, and even after all these years, it still makes me sad. To help with this, before we break into groups, I remind my students that this project will last a few days, and it's not a marriage that will (hopefully) last forever. I encourage them to invite some people into their group who they haven't worked with previously. You will generally have a student or two who understands the deeper meaning behind your words, and who will make sure that everyone who wants a group gets a group. At the same time, sometimes students simply prefer to work alone. This hack is about personalizing the learning, and if that is what works best for that student, you will want to respect that as well.

There is no way I can personalize the learning for every student. Actually, you can. But it means giving up some of the control over the class. See, the key element to personalized learning is providing students with options, and often, this means allowing *them* the chance to create an assignment that best fits their needs. It's not as scary as it sounds. You can still set the learning target and parameters of the assignment, but you must be willing to let your students find their own ways of reaching that target.

Students won't get anything done if they work with their friends. This is a fairly common concern with this hack. After all, we are talking about kids here, right? But think about this: Do you work harder for your friends or for people you don't know? My guess is your friends, and the same holds true for your students. Letting your students self-select their partners won't weaken the groups, it will *solidify* them. Give it a try.

This sounds like more work for me. You got me on this one. Yes, it will require more work, initially, from you. But once you line up an array of options, the increased levels of engagement will more than make up for the time you spend front-loading the learning. Plus, teaching becomes much more fun when students are excited about your class, and the ideas in this hack will create positive energy. So rather than looking at it as more work, look at it as an investment that will pay big dividends later!

THE HACK IN ACTION

Student Maddy Frech has experienced personalized learning first-hand, and she is a big proponent of its use. "It is important for teachers to allow their students to have appropriate, personalized learning in the classroom because it gets students to enjoy what is happening in class. Oftentimes, students detest learning and school simply because it's so boring. But when teachers give students some choice in the learning, it almost becomes fun! There are so many examples of when I have been so into an assignment that I didn't want to actually leave the classroom!"

One of her favorite assignments was a music parody video she helped choreograph based around the Civil War. Frech, who has spent years dancing both within and outside of school, was allowed the opportunity to blend her passion for dance with her academic life. "I loved this activity so much that I actually put in way more time and effort than was required. It not only prepared me for the final exam, but I was actually excited to take the test so I could show off what I had learned!"

She says that the benefits of personalized learning extend far beyond academics. "When teachers provide fun activities and experiences, students not only start to appreciate the class and the lesson, but also the teacher. Students are excited to walk into a class that they know will be engaging, and they will work harder and behave better for teachers who give them those chances. Plus, when you are having fun doing something, it's a lot harder to get off task."

A well-behaved class where students are having fun as they learn? How many of us would be fine with that?

In *Freedom Writers*, first-year teacher Erin Gruwell was in desperate need of finding ways to help her students learn. Like many teachers, both beginners and veterans, she entered the classroom with a teaching plan that she assumed would work. The problem was, she was making those assumptions based on who she thought her students *would be* rather than on who they actually *were*.

After several tough weeks, Ms. Gruwell inadvertently began to personalize the learning for her students when she started to talk to them about their lives, and as a result, she began to find success. She began to do pre-assessments to see what her students knew, she created an ungraded journal assignment for her students to share their thoughts, and she allowed them to do self-assessments. Reflection became a regular part of the class environment, and she herself constantly looked for new ways to present the curriculum. In the end, because of the personalized connection she made through her teaching, she was able to look her students in the eyes each day and tell them, "I see who you are."

From my experience, when I have made the effort to personalize the learning for my students, they have consistently exceeded my expectations. It helps me target their learning more precisely, and allows them to become active participants in their learning. It's effective, it's meaningful, and it's engaging. Now it's your turn to find out how *your* students learn best.

REASSESS HOW YOU ASSESS

The Benefits of Self-Assessment and Self-Grading

HACK 7

Test scores and measures of achievement tell you where a student is, but they don't tell you where a student could end up.
– CAROL S. DWECK, EDUCATOR AND AUTHOR

THE PROBLEM: TEACHERS GRADE LIKE THEY ALWAYS HAVE

STOP ME IF you've heard this one before. It's test day. Your students clear everything off their desks, and they proceed to take an exam to see if they understand the material that they've been studying for the past couple of weeks. When they finish, the students turn in their tests, and the next lesson begins. A few days later (after lugging the tests to and from school multiple times), you hand the tests back to your students with a grade or percentage at the top. At this point, you may or may not do a quick overview of the test, explaining the answers to a couple of commonly missed questions. But after a few minutes and a handful of clarifications, it's time to get back on track with the current unit. Sound familiar?

The world we live in has undergone quite a drastic change in the last fifty years (I still remember how excited I was when we finally got a VCR!), but for whatever reason, how we grade and assess student work hasn't really been updated very much in that time. In fact, I don't think it would be a stretch to say that the way many teachers grade and assess assignments today is probably fairly similar to how *their* teachers graded and assessed their work when they were in school. And to me, that's messed up.

THE HACK: REASSESS HOW YOU ASSESS

That's why this hack centers on the importance of letting your students take some ownership in their assessments. The concept of classroom management extends far beyond reactive measures intended to calm down a situation. In fact, the best classroom management strategies focus on ideas that cut off those situations before they arise, and letting your students have a voice in the grading process can help accomplish this. If students have a clear understanding of how the assessment process works, or even better, have a *role* in that process, the likelihood of them causing a disruption as a result of a misunderstanding is cut dramatically.

Disruptions are often caused by unclear explanations (the assignment, the rules, the grade), and this hack will help provide students with transparency regarding how the grading process works. In addition, this hack allows students to reflect and engage in their learning rather than passively standing by waiting for you to assess the outcome *of* their learning. Students often feel intimidated by concepts they don't understand, and as a result, they act out as a way to deflect attention away from their academic shortcomings. But when they are given the opportunity to openly reflect and question the learning, they become more involved in wanting to understand the ideas and concepts being presented.

 One of the biggest hurdles for students to get over initially is the idea that being wrong is bad.

You can find a wide range of methods that incorporate student input into the grading process, each with its own logic and benefit. Here are some strategies to encourage students to take a leading role in assessment.

Self-assessment. Allowing students to self-assess gives them the chance to reflect on the strengths and weaknesses of their individual learning. This is in stark contrast to traditional grading, which often has students comparing themselves based against what others have learned. Additionally, students are more willing to be authentic in their assessment since they themselves are the ones judging the product quality. The result is that students are willing to work harder for the sake of learning rather than for the grade.

I use self-assessment in a variety of ways, but regardless of whether it's for a writing assignment, a project, or a participation grade, the method is pretty similar.

1. Provide a rubric or verbally identify the learning targets and expectations of the assignment to make sure everyone is on the same page prior to the assessment.

2. After answering any clarifying questions, have students self-assess their work based on the guidelines.

3. Have students write a brief overview (three to five sentences) explaining why they feel their work reflects the score they gave themselves.

4. Students turn in their assessments.

5. Review student assessments, making additional comments when necessary.

I love letting students self-assess simply because it provides them with the opportunity to tell me what they *do* understand rather than me showing them what they *don't* understand. Plus, it breaks down the power struggle between teachers and students that often stems from grades, and this ultimately results in a more positive classroom experience.

Self-grading/discussion-based grading. Self-grading (also called discussion-based grading) is different than self-assessment in that it is used more often on summative assessments like tests, and self-assessment is used more on formative assessments like those identified above. In essence, this one is more teacher-driven and is used when there is typically one correct answer. From my perspective, tests should be used not only to assess the learning that has previously taken place, but also to guide where the learning goes next. Allowing students to self-grade provides them with an opportunity to ask questions about the test (solidifying their understanding), and supplies you with a better understanding of where they are in relation to the learning goals and, perhaps more important, where they should go next.

It works like this. After completing a test, I ask students to take out their red pens for grading. For the next several minutes, we grade the test together, with students grading their own tests. I read the question, then ask for students to volunteer an answer. This is where the discussion portion comes into play. This type of Q and A keeps the class engaged in the learning and allows them to ask clarifying questions. The result is that students not only understand why an answer is right, they also discover why an answer is wrong (which, if you think about it, is just as important). This is a concept that is overlooked when the typical teacher-graded test is handed back. Plus, this system allows for students to explain their thought process to me in a way that a circled letter on a multiple-choice test just can't do. Finally, you can add an extra layer to the learning by asking follow-up questions.

Peer review to self-assessment. In the peer review to self-assessment model, students create a self-assessment based in part on the comments created by their peers. These types of assessments work best on projects or written work, and they are a great way for students to get an array of opinions on their work prior to judging it themselves. The process looks like this:

Direct every student to take out a piece of paper and create a T-chart across the top. Label the two sections with a plus (+) and a minus (-). Students will leave this paper, along with a pen, next to the assignment at their desk.

1. After discussing the required elements of the assignment, students walk around the room and assess two of their classmates' projects based on the stated criteria. As they assess the work, they are to write two positive comments (in the + column) and two suggestions for improvement (in the - column) on the T-chart next to the assignment.

2. Once they have completed one assessment, they stand up and wait for a seat to open, where they repeat the process.

3. After assessing the work of two classmates, students return to their desks to read the comments made regarding their projects.

4. After reading the comments, students write a self-assessment (on the same sheet that their peers commented on) where they explain why they feel they deserve the score they gave themselves. I ask them to provide specific examples, both positive and negative, that show me why this project warrants the score it received.

5. Once they complete the score and the self-assessment, students write their names on the assessment sheet and turn it in.

6. The teacher then does a final assessment, adjusting any scores as needed.

One important point of distinction is to make sure you don't confuse peer assessments with peer editing or peer grading. The peer review to self-assessment *does not* have students edit or grade their peers' work, but rather has them comment on the content of the work. So rather than focusing on the small details (punctuation, spelling) like peer edits often do, peer reviews instead comment on the big details (organization, flow). From my experience, feedback like this *about* a paper is much more powerful than random marks written *on* a paper.

The peer review to self-assessment is a great classroom

management tool in that it allows students to be involved in the grading process in a self-paced manner. Depending on the size of the project, I usually allow about five minutes per review, and then add an additional five minutes for the self-assessment. All told, if you have students review the work of two classmates, this process should take less than twenty minutes.

WHAT YOU CAN DO TOMORROW

The best classroom management strategies are easy to implement and have immediate buy-in from the students. Each of the following strategies allows students to understand *how* to assess their work, and more important, *why* they earned their score.

- **TALK TO YOUR CLASS ABOUT SELF-ASSESSMENTS.** Initially, this concept might feel strange to students who are used to the teachers having all the say in the grading process. Explain to them how it works, and provide them with the opportunity to ask questions about the benefits.

- **DEBATE THE PROS AND CONS.** To help students better understand how it works, ask them to write down and discuss the pros and cons of self-assessments. This can be done in small or large groups. This is a great opportunity to let students get up and write their ideas on the board (see Hack 4).

- **DO A TURN-N-TALK ABOUT STRENGTHS AND WEAKNESSES.** A simple way to introduce self-assessments is to have students do a quick turn-n-talk (see Hack 4) about their personal strengths and weaknesses. I usually model this by identifying one of my own strengths and weaknesses. When they get into groups, I ask students to explain one strength and one weakness that they recognize in themselves. This gives them a little more comfort with the logic behind self-reflection, and this practice will pay benefits later when they must self-reflect on a project.

- **HAVE STUDENTS SELF-ASSESS THEIR EFFORT.** As students leave your class, request that they self-assess their overall effort in class. I ask them to think about their participation, attitude, and engagement with the learning. This can be done as an exit ticket, or you can have them "high five" their ratings as they walk out the door. I usually provide three options— Green = Awesome, Yellow = As Expected, and Red = I'll Do Better Tomorrow—but you can provide as many levels as you feel are appropriate. Either method serves as an effective, low-stakes opportunity for your students to be reflective about their work. (See Act 7: High Five Hands.)

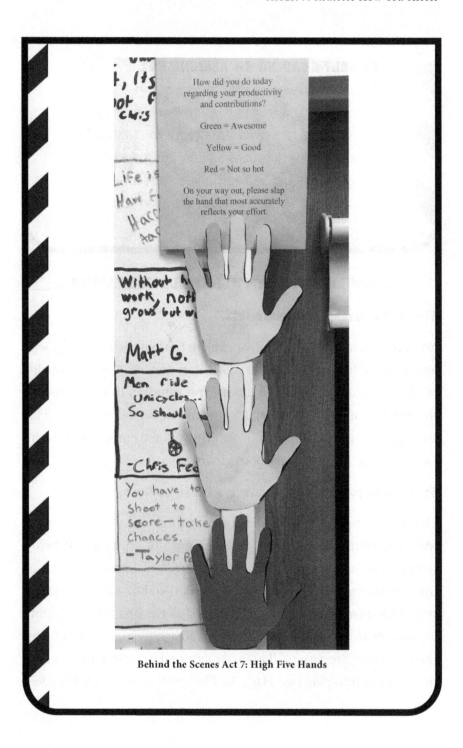

Behind the Scenes Act 7: High Five Hands

> • **TRY SELF-GRADING AN ASSIGNMENT.** If you have a homework assignment or a small quiz due in class, give self-grading a shot. If executed well, this type of grading should run similar to a discussion, with follow-up and clarifying questions asked throughout. As you do this, you should be hearing your students' voices just as often, if not more frequently, than your own.

A BLUEPRINT FOR FULL IMPLEMENTATION

Step 1: Research self-assessments.

You can find many resources that explain the logic behind using self-assessments. In *Hacking Assessment*, Starr Sackstein offers a wealth of ideas to promote a shift in assessment mindset, to foster student involvement in assessment, and to maximize digital resources. Flip through the research, and see if you think these could improve the learning (and thus the classroom environment).

Step 2: Let your students know it's OK to be wrong.

One of the biggest hurdles for students to get over initially is the idea that being wrong is bad. While I am not arguing that being wrong is by any means ideal, students need to know that part of understanding why something is right is the ability to understand why something else is wrong. This hack works best when students let their guards down and aren't afraid to ask for clarity about why their answers are wrong. This is where making personal connections comes into play (see Hack 3). The more comfortable they feel around you as a person, the more likely they are to take this risk as a student.

Step 3: Continue the discussion about self-assessments.

The key to effectively implementing this hack lies in the clarity and consistency with which you present it. Stress the trust that you are placing in them, and let them know exactly what the expectations are each time you try this.

Step 4: Commit to full implementation.

Letting students reflect on their learning is a valuable skill that remains useful throughout school and beyond. Additionally, once they understand how to do it properly, your class will become a place where all students are engaged in the learning process.

OVERCOMING PUSHBACK

Adopting a new approach to grading, especially when the old system has been used for decades, can be a hard sell. To help gain support for these ideas, here are answers to a few of the common concerns about this hack.

What if students are totally off-base with their assessments? This is a serious concern that most likely will happen, especially when you first introduce this concept. Grades are a major stressor for students, and some will see this type of grading as an opportunity to inflate their scores. I offset this by letting students know that if what I see in their work doesn't jive with the grade they give themselves, we will have a "clarifying" discussion. That in itself limits the grade inflators. In fact, students are often too harsh on themselves. This, too, warrants a conversation. In the end, after discussing it, we come to an agreement about what the score should be and why it deserves that grade. This clarification of the expectations then serves as a guide for the student when doing future self-assessments.

I need to use the time in class for teaching, not grading. In my view, class time should be used for *learning*, and this hack provides opportunities for that. Whether it is through reflection (self-assessment), discussion (self-grading/discussion-based grading), or analysis (peer review to self-assessment), learning definitely plays a key role in the implementation of this hack. Additionally, these strategies allow both you and your students to better understand the learning that has occurred. As a result, you will be able to more accurately target your next unit.

I'm fine with students self-assessing, but I don't feel comfortable letting students assess each other. Remember, any time students look at the work of their peers, they are *reviewing* their work, not *assessing* it. They don't edit the work in *any* way, but instead they comment on the strengths and weaknesses of the assignment. Like many benefits of this hack, this process allows students to see what others think of their work, thus giving them a more solid foundation from which to base their own assessment.

THE HACK IN ACTION

Katie Schwab, a veteran second-grade teacher, recently made the switch to a more student-led assessment style, and says she's been amazed by the results. While initially uncertain about how it might work, she soon discovered that there are many ways to have students assess themselves. As she started trying different assessment methods, it quickly became clear that the biggest difference between her old method and the new one was in the motivation of her students.

"I have jars with the various learning targets on them, and kids put their name sticks in the jar that best illustrates where they think they are in terms of meeting that target at any given moment. I have baskets with 'not yet,' 'almost,' and 'got it,' and students put their work where they think it should go. They also talk about their learning much more frequently now, and they immediately know what their strengths and weaknesses are," Schwab says.

"Kids no longer are completing tasks to please me, but instead are doing it to please themselves. The ownership of giving yourself the grade is quite motivating. And, as a result of our learning targets, it is *very* clear what they are working toward. With the old system, 'Pleasing Ms. Katie' was pretty ambiguous!" She also noticed an improvement in engagement and classroom management, and says that her kids are much more engaged now because they understand the purpose behind each and every thing they do. This better understanding of the learning process has resulted in a classroom that runs much smoother than before. She does note, however, that setting up this atmosphere takes time and patience.

Schwab took the ideas of this hack even further during parent/teacher conferences, and offered student-led conferences. "The kids were able to show their parents an assignment against a learning target and clearly state where they were doing well and what they still needed to work on." Schwab is excited to seek out new ways for her students to grow as learners. "I love how assessments like these allow students to embrace challenges and become more comfortable with making mistakes and learning from them. It's like magic!"

So let me ask you this: When was the last time you lugged home a bunch of papers and had it feel like magic? If it's been awhile (if ever), then it might be time to shake up your grading system.

Minerva McGonagall, the transfiguration professor at Hogwarts School of Witchcraft and Wizardry, knows a thing or two about creating magic in the classroom. Throughout the *Harry Potter* series, Professor McGonagall exemplified what it meant to get her students involved in the learning and assessment process. Her lessons—from teaching Ron Weasley to dance and transforming animals into water droplets—centered on providing students with an awareness of *what* they were learning and a clear understanding of *why* they were learning it. By engaging her students in this manner, Professor McGonagall modeled that the application of learning far outweighed mere content knowledge.

This approach gave all her students, from Hermione Granger to Neville Longbottom, a part in the learning process, and also allowed them to recognize their strengths and weaknesses regarding the topic. Additionally, she encouraged her students to experiment with their ideas as a way to assess whether or not they had reached the learning target. At the culminating scene of the series, she told Seamus Finnigan to use his "particular proclivity for pyrotechnics" to make the bridge leading to Hogwarts go "Boom!" to keep Voldemort from reaching Hogwarts, and in doing so, provided a real-world application to the learning previously done in class. Time and again, Professor McGonagall showed that teachers are rather good at magic, and that this magic can be shared with students by guiding them through the learning process and recognizing their strengths.

Grades can cause a great deal of stress for both teachers and students, and this hack helps to alleviate much of it by making the grading process more transparent for everyone involved. When students play an active role in the assessment system, they better understand *what* they learned and *why* they learned it, so they can apply their learning to real life. Simply put, they begin to focus on the learning rather than solely looking at the score at the top of the paper.

EMAIL EARLY,
EMAIL OFTEN

The Value of Positive
Communication

HACK 8

*Kind words can be short and easy to speak,
but their echoes are truly endless.*
— MOTHER TERESA, CATHOLIC NUN

THE PROBLEM: TEACHERS OFTEN ONLY
REPORT THE NEGATIVE STUFF

AS TEACHERS, WE do more than our fair share of communicating during the school day. The vast majority of this communication is directed at our students, and it is primarily done during and around our classes. These interactions are often informal, and more times than not, they are friendly and positive in nature.

So why, then, is this hack's problem titled "Teachers often only report the negative stuff"? Because now I invite you to think about the last few emails or phone conversations you had with a parent or an administrator about a student. Were these friendly and positive, or were they negative and pointing out something bad that the student had done? And what about your recent conversations with colleagues about students? Were you talking about a great idea that a student shared, or were you venting about that kid who never shuts up?

 Whenever talking about a student, try to incorporate at least one positive comment sometime during the conversation.

For whatever reason, while the vast majority of our conversations with students are positive and encouraging in tone, it seems as though the opposite holds true when discussing our students with parents, colleagues, and administrators. Oftentimes, it appears as if all we share via email is bad news. It's important to remember that these emails, while meaningful, hold a power that extends beyond the words. In fact, parents and students (and do I daresay teachers?) will often pay more attention to the perceived *tone* of the message than the message itself. As a result, this unintended negativity can really disrupt your relationships with students and their parents.

But the opposite can hold true for positive emails. Rather than having students dread coming to your class after an email that pointed out their flaws, what if you could create excitement in students because of emails that praised them? Think that might improve the classroom environment? This hack will show you how to do that, and all in less than five minutes per day.

THE HACK: EMAIL EARLY, EMAIL OFTEN

We all recognize the value that technology provides for our classes, and yet for whatever reason, many of us still don't use email to its full potential. Sure, we use it to confirm meetings, read agendas, and post announcements. We also tend to break it out when a student fails a test, throws an item across the room, or makes inappropriate comments in class.

But how often do we use it to *improve* our classroom atmosphere? There are many ways to use email to strengthen the classroom environment, each with its own benefit. The three examples listed below allow you to start the year on a positive note, solidify it as the year progresses, and finish the year on an upward trajectory.

Beginning-of-the-year emails. At the beginning of the year, send an email to parents, introduce yourself, and ask them to send you five little-known facts about their child. As you begin to receive these, read them aloud to the class, but do so without using the child's name or gender. After reading each one, have the class try to guess who the email is about. Read two per day until all the emails have been read. (See Act 8: Parent Email.)

Hello Parents,

Welcome to 8th grade English! As a way to get to know your child better, I need your help. Here's the scoop…

Please email me five little-known facts about your child. **Please do not use your child's name in your description!** Detail things like his/her hobbies, talents, and accomplishments. If possible, try to include items that your child may not share with many people.

I will be reading these letters out loud, and the class will try to figure out who it is based on your description. This is a great opportunity for you to brag about (and maybe embarrass) your child a little. Also, please do not tell your child what you're writing! This assignment works best when he/she gets to hear it for the first time in class.

I will begin reading these on the first day of school, and I will continue reading them until they run out! And when you respond, if you could please include your child's name in the subject line of the email, that would really help me keep things organized.

Thanks in advance for taking part in this assignment. The kids always love this, and we (the class and me) really get to know one another better as a result of your participation.

Looking forward to a great year!

Thanks,

Mike Roberts

Behind the Scenes Act 8: Parent Email

This activity serves two purposes. First, it makes your initial contact with parents a positive one. This establishes your relationship with them by starting the year on the right footing. Second, it builds a sense of community within your class, one that will help solidify the relationships with and among your students. And as evidenced throughout the previous hacks, strong rapport generally equates to fewer classroom management issues.

Two positive emails a day. At the end of each day, send out two emails where you identify various positive activities that you saw from your students. This can include a student doing well on a test, working hard in class, helping to clean up, or just bringing a friendly attitude to class. If it's something good, it's fair game!

These emails should be sent to a variety of recipients including parents, administrators, and colleagues (including counselors and advisors), and they should be used as a way to recognize the good deeds that students do on a daily basis. And always remember to copy the student on the email. Also, be sure to follow up with the student the next day to make sure they know that you are proud of what they did.

These quick emails can be very powerful in strengthening your relationships with students and parents. Sending a positive message shows them that you care about the child as a person, not just as a student. Plus, from a personal perspective, it allows you to walk out the door focused on the positive experiences from the day rather than the all-to-frequent negative stressors that often come home with us.

One quick tip about this one: "Copy and paste" is your friend! For example, if a student does well on a test, I usually shoot out an email saying that I am super proud of her effort. But what if five students do really well on a test? There is no need to come up with five different ways of saying the same thing. Your words still have the same sentiment behind them, regardless of whether they are aimed at one student or a thousand. If you mean it, send it—just make sure to change the name and pronouns!

End-of-the-year emails. It is also valuable to get parents involved at the end of the year—just as you did with the email at the beginning of the year. Rather than asking for unusual facts, ask parents to share their thoughts about how their child has grown over the course of the school year. Again, read about two per day leading up to the end of the year. And while I used to ask parents to include the child's name as a way to celebrate the student's growth, my class convinced me that trying to guess who is being talked about (like the beginning-of-the-year email) is much more fun. This is a perfect way to wrap up the year by partnering with parents to praise the positive traits and experiences of their child. And seriously, what parents are going to turn down a chance to brag about their children?

Now don't get me wrong. These emails should by no means replace all of the friendly and enthusiastic conversations you have with your students each and every day. Instead, emails like these should be used to *supplement* those valuable conversations. Because the truth of the matter is, while we all cherish those one-on-one conversations, we also sometimes like to get recognized on a little larger stage, and a simple email can make that happen.

WHAT YOU CAN DO TOMORROW

Creating a positive communication channel between you, the parents, and the student doesn't have to be a long, complicated endeavor. In fact, all it takes is a little awareness and a few minutes per day.

- **PAY ATTENTION TO THE GOOD STUFF THAT YOUR STUDENTS DO.** Your students do amazing acts each and every day, yet too often we fail to give credit where credit is due. Start searching out and recognizing those everyday acts of

kindness that happen in and around your classroom on a daily basis, like holding the door open
for someone, picking up a classmates' pen, or even
simply saying thank you to the teacher. These are
all acts that, in the big picture, deserve recognition.
These activities are happening; now it's up to you
to notice.

- **INCLUDE AT LEAST ONE POSITIVE COMMENT
  WHEN TALKING ABOUT YOUR STUDENTS.**
  Whenever you're talking about a student, try to
  incorporate at least one positive comment sometime during the conversation. It's easy to jump on
  the bandwagon in the faculty lounge or at a team
  meeting when talking about the shortcomings of
  a student. Try to turn the conversation around by
  offering up some of the student's positive traits.
  Doing so will not only redirect the tone of the
  conversation, but it will also put you in a better
  mindset the next time you see that student.

- **SEND TWO POSITIVE EMAILS.** As outlined above,
  start tomorrow and send two positive emails to celebrate the awesome things your students did today.

A BLUEPRINT FOR FULL IMPLEMENTATION

Step 1: Send an email to your *students* the week before school starts and introduce yourself.

Sending an email to your students prior to school serves many purposes. First, it gives you a chance to introduce yourself to your students in a casual manner. Next, it provides your students with a chance to ask any last-minute questions before starting class. This can potentially alleviate the first-day anxiety suffered by some students. Finally, it shows your students that you are excited to meet them and for school to get started.

Step 2: Send an email to *parents* and provide a little background about yourself.

The purpose of this email is similar to the student email except that it gives more of your professional background and teaching philosophy. This gives parents some insight into who you are and what you stand for. You definitely don't want to get too deep into this, and a quick overview should more than suffice. This is also an easy place to ask parents to provide you with five interesting facts about their child (as discussed earlier). Having a few of these ready to go on Day One will give you a great activity to start off the year.

Step 3: Create a running log of the kind acts that students do.

There are numerous acts of kindness that happen within our schools every day, but they often get lost or forgotten as a result of our hectic daily schedule. A simple way to keep these organized is to maintain a running log with the student's name, date, and a brief description of the act. This can be a digital document that you keep on your computer or an old-school spiral notebook that you write in. Either way, taking a few notes at the end of each class will keep you from forgetting the awesomeness you see each and every day.

Step 4: Keep parents and the principal in the loop.

While sending home a positive email about a test or an assignment is great, parents also love to hear about the non-academic aspects of their child. Emailing about how their child performed a kind act or improved in class participation shows parents that you recognize and appreciate their child as more than just a percentage in the grade book. These also serve as building blocks for if/when you have to send that difficult email later. In addition, principals are sometimes in the dark about what goes on from day to day in the classroom. Hearing from you will help them become aware of situations that they can't see for themselves. Plus, focusing on the positive aspects of your class shows that you take pride in your students' success. Always make sure to copy the student.

Step 5: Send an end-of-the-year email asking about student growth.

These parent emails are a great way to look at how students have grown in all aspects of their lives, and the messages can focus on what the child has *learned* rather than on the grade that they *earned*. It's also just a really fun way to wind down the school year.

OVERCOMING PUSHBACK

The beauty of this hack is in its simplicity. It can be done quickly, and can easily be applied within any class, regardless of grade level or subject. But like anything else, some people might have concerns about trying this out. Here are possible responses:

I don't have time for this. Let's be real here. We are talking about five minutes or less per day! Try it and you'll see that it's a very small amount of time compared to a very large return on investment.

Some of my families don't have email. This is a legitimate concern, but one that is becoming less and less common as technology continues to grow. The solution to this would be to either call the parent or send a hard copy/note home with the student. The downside to these alternatives is that it's sometimes difficult to reach parents by phone, and notes, well, they don't always seem to make it to their final destination.

What about the student whose parents don't respond? I generally don't get concerned if I don't hear back from a parent regarding a positive email that I randomly sent. And actually, I am amazed at how many parents *do* email me back. But the beginning- and end-of-the-year emails are a pretty big deal, and if I don't hear back from parents (after a few reminders), I usually ask the student if they would like to write up something on their own. If not, I will ask them if it is OK for me to write it up for them. Finally, if they refuse both offers, I give them the chance to opt out of this activity. But for the record, I can count on my two hands the number of kids who have chosen to completely withdraw from this.

I talk to parents at parent/teacher conferences. Isn't that enough? Simply put, no. Meeting two, maybe even three, times per year falls far short in keeping parents connected with what is happening. To me, parent/teacher conferences are the equivalent of newspapers pre-internet—the only option at the time. But in today's instant-access society, parent/teacher conferences just don't cut it by themselves. Of course, the face-to-face time is valuable, but email messages are a timely and effective addition to your parent communications.

I already leave comments on assignments via my grading

system. While this is good, comments like these seem less personal than an email. Plus, while I know students often read these comments, parents generally don't. Additionally, younger students often don't turn in assignments via programs like these, and they deserve just as much recognition for the positive acts they do as the older students.

THE HACK IN ACTION

Parent Jill Lang is a big believer in the role that email can serve in creating a strong bond among the teacher, the parents, and the student. Lang is especially fond of the beginning-of-the-year email that asked her to share her parental insights about her child. She explains that the introductory email "allowed the teacher to get to know my son on a more personalized level. He asked questions about who my child was, including wanting to know what his favorite sports are, what he likes to do in his free time, and any secret talents he might have. By doing this, I felt confident that the teacher had a true interest in my child as a person, not just as a student." Lang continues by adding, "I guess more than anything else, it just put me at ease and assured me that the teacher had a vested interest in my child."

Lang further adds that regular email communication throughout the year can have academic benefits as well. "My son's teacher did a great job of updating me on what he was seeing at school. Regardless of whether it was for a test, an assignment, or a behavioral issue, I always appreciated getting an email every so often that shared a part of my son that I couldn't get at home. The ability to know what was going on inside the classroom allowed me to support my son both personally and academically in a much clearer fashion. For me, I just don't feel like two parent/teacher conferences can adequately address everything that happens over the course of the year, and emails like these serve as a springboard for open dialogue to continue throughout the school year." And while these emails may have to address tough situations at times, when problems do arise, Lang points out that "parents are more willing to work with the teacher and devise a game plan to resolve the problem as a result of the positive foundation set earlier in the year." Lang concludes by saying, "Email communication, starting with the introduction email and continuing throughout the year, allowed both my son and me to have a dialogue with the teacher that reflected on *all* areas of my son's growth. Because of this, it just seemed like fewer things fell through the cracks."

Perhaps no recently released movie showcases the importance of communication better than *Step.* In this documentary, students, parents, teachers, and administrators all worked tirelessly toward the same objective of getting the senior members of this all-girl Baltimore step team into college. Dancer Tayla Solomon's mother intervened when Tayla's grades begin to slip, counselor Paula Dofat made it her mission to ensure that each and every one of them graduated from college, and coach Gari McIntyre instilled that what they were doing was way bigger than step. She said, "It's about sacrifice, not making excuses, [and] a positive attitude."

A consistent stream of communication flows between the school, the students, and the parents, and helps push students to their full potential. They say it takes a village to raise a child, and the dedication of this school community illustrated the impor-tance of relationships and communication on students' success.

While I understand that parents can be challenging, I encourage you to give this hack a try and see how it works for you, your students, their parents, and school administrators. If there is one thing that parents love to do, it's to hear (and talk) about the good their child has done. Sending emails and consistent communica-tions is an easy way for you to make this happen.

FIST BUMPS, HIGH FIVES, AND SHOUT-OUTS

Starting and Ending Class the Right Way

HACK 9

*Give people high fives just for getting out of
bed. Being a person is hard sometimes.*
— KID PRESIDENT, ACTOR

THE PROBLEM: THE BEGINNING AND ENDING OF CLASS ARE OFTEN WASTED

THINK ABOUT THE beginning and ending of your last class. And I don't mean the moment you started teaching until the second you ended. I mean what did your class look like when the bell both started and ended your class?

This is how mine looked for the first several years of my career, and perhaps your class looks like this too: The bell would ring to start class, and I would wait a couple minutes before "officially" starting to allow time for the stragglers to come in. My logic was that I didn't want to start a lesson only to have it get interrupted, let alone have to repeat what I just said for those who showed up late. So rather than jumping right in, I'd let my students chat quietly as I caught up on a few emails or took attendance. Finally, after everyone had arrived, I'd begin class by giving an overview of the day.

 A high five can be given out for even the smallest act. It's a quick, cheap, and effective way to keep students in a positive mindset during class.

Meanwhile, a similar scenario held true for the last two minutes of my class. After a long lesson, students (and generally me, too) were ready to move on, and all too often I fell back onto the "work quietly until the bell rings" mantra as a way to wrap things up. At this point, much like the beginning of class, the last few minutes would slowly erode away as my students worked quietly in small groups and I returned to my desk to do some grading or input scores.

Not exactly the kind of exemplary scenario you see in the movies, eh? (At least not from the good teachers.) But after years of letting minutes slip away on a daily basis, I slowly began to realize that this time could serve as a valuable and impactful part of class. And while two minutes here or there might not sound like much in the big picture, at the time, it represented nearly 10 percent of my class period. *Ten percent!* After realizing this, I knew that I needed to change how I used those intro and closing minutes.

THE HACK: FIST BUMPS, HIGH FIVES, AND SHOUT-OUTS

After wasting all that time for way too long, I now consider those four minutes as the most important minutes of my entire class period. Now before I go any further, let me emphasize that I didn't say that those four minutes are the most important *teaching* minutes of my class period. In fact, the four minutes I'm talking about generally have little to do with the content we are addressing that day. And that's why they are so important to classroom management.

Think about it. Depending on the length of your classes, students often spend between forty-five and ninety minutes engulfed in the content of your class. And to complicate it even more, they will follow up your class by doing that exact same thing (albeit in another subject) *multiple times per day*!

When I first started looking into changing my teaching approach, I couldn't help but think of each class period as its own little workout that focused on a different part of the brain. And as many of us know, working out too hard for too long often leads to burnout. That's why warming up and cooling down are so important to a workout. The warmup allows your body to slowly build up to the stress of a workout, and the cool-down helps to slowly drop the level of exertion from the session back to a normal range. And thus began the two-minute warmup and cool-down concepts for my classroom.

Now, if I'm being honest, when I first started this, I was doing it simply to give myself a chance to breathe. But as this concept slowly developed, I began to realize that, in addition to giving me and my students a little much-needed downtime, these minutes could also serve as a valuable tool in helping me build and maintain my relationship with my class. So rather than just letting them talk as I was busy working at my desk, I decided to connect with them in a way that was somehow missing during our class discussions. And it worked.

Here's a quick peek into how the warmup and cool-down sessions work. As students enter my room, I usually greet them at the door with a fist bump, a smile, and a "what up?" This simple act sets a positive tone for the day and allows me the opportunity to gauge how my students are doing prior to the beginning of class. For example, if a student comes in looking a bit down, talking with them for a few seconds will give me insight into what's happening before we dive into the daily grind of class. This, in turn, will help me better understand why they might not be as engaged as usual that day. These quick conversations, which generally only last a few seconds, are a simple way for me to diagnose my students' moods before I start teaching.

After the bell rings, I move from the doorway into my class, thus beginning the two-minute warmup. (There are numerous names for these types of activities, including starters, do-now, and bell-ringers.) And while this is an informal and soft start to my class, it serves a purpose in that it prepares students to be productive by easing them into the learning in an engaging and enjoyable way. This helps them buy in to what is happening, and as a result, they are much quicker to jump on board with the lessons. And while teachers need to find warmup activities that work for them and their classes, here is a list of my daily warmup activities that you are welcome to use or adapt.

Monday: Good Weekend/Bad Weekend. This concept is pretty simple. For one minute or so, I ask students to share all the good things that happened to them the prior weekend. This allows students the chance to show the class (and me) pieces of their personal lives that we might not otherwise know about. Activities like family events and hobbies are often discussed during this time, and it definitely starts class in the right direction.

Once the good parts have been talked about, we turn our

attention to the not-so-good parts. Again, students often share personal details here, including stuff that is challenging and troubling. And while this idea might make some teachers uncomfortable, I encourage you to look at these issues in a positive light. After all, if a student is willing to share with you that a family member died or that they got grounded for the weekend, it shows that they have a trust in you that goes beyond the standard teacher role.

Tuesday: Tip of the Week. For this warmup, I provide my class with an important life lesson. This is a great opportunity to teach the "hidden" curriculum by touching on topics like perseverance, friendship, and creativity. I write it on the "Tip of the Week Board," and it remains there for the entire week. I then try to point out examples throughout the week when students have put the tip into action. Additionally, I always include a video element to showcase or support the tip. YouTube is a great source for these (see Hack 5), and it also provides you with links to similar videos.

I often share the topic of the upcoming Tip of the Week (but not the suggestion itself), and I let students know that I am open to any videos they might suggest that reflect this idea. This, again, gives them some ownership in the process, and thus helps to build a solid foundation for a positive classroom atmosphere. The last step of the Tip of the Week is to have students explain to a partner how the video or they themselves relate to the tip. This is my favorite part of this activity, and let me tell you, be ready to hear some seriously strong insights! (See Act 9: Tip of the Week—Sample Ideas and Videos.)

Tip of the Week
Sample Ideas and Videos

Tip – Be the hero of your own movie.
YouTube Video - "Joe Rogan: Be the Hero of Your Own Movie"

Tip – Have big goals, but don't lose sight of the small things.
YouTube Video - "Test Your Awareness: Do the Test"

Tip – Be creative in whatever you do.
YouTube Video - "SWA Rap"

Tip – A little gesture can mean a lot.
YouTube Video - "Free Hugs Campaign - Official Page"

Tip – Do awesome things in your life.
YouTube Video - "People Are Awesome 2013 Hadouken"

Tip – Find your greatness.
YouTube Video - "Nike: Find Your Greatness - Jogger"

Tip – It's OK to draw outside the lines every now and then.
YouTube Video – "JK Wedding Entrance Dance"

Behind the Scenes Act 9: Tip of the Week – Sample Ideas and Videos

Wednesday: Failure and Growth – As students walk in on Wednesday, I ask them to reflect on anything they might have failed at over the previous week. This can be any issue, including academics (didn't keep up on homework), friendships (said mean words), or athletics (lost a game). These failures can be expressed verbally (with a partner), digitally (on a Google Doc), or in written format (in a journal). Once students have reflected on their failures, I ask them to explain what they learned from this and how they can grow as a result. This self-reflection (see Hack 7) helps students realize that mistakes are a part of life, and the value comes from what we learn as a result.

Thursday: Thankful Thursday – In today's world, it is easy to complain about what we *don't* have, and if you have spent any time around kids, you know they are experts at this. And rather than complaining about how unfair the world is or what they didn't get for their birthday, Thankful Thursday helps student think about what they *do* have that is good in their lives. Like the Failure and Growth activity, this can include reflecting on a wide range of both personal and academic issues, and it helps students appreciate many simple, everyday things that they often take for granted.

Friday: The Week in Haiku – After a long week at school, nothing wraps things up better than a week-in-review Haiku! Using the standard five-seven-five syllable count, students will amaze you with their poetic abilities. I recommend modeling this by creating a class haiku or two before just setting them loose on their own (this is especially true for younger elementary grades). These short, insightful poems are a great way to gain a little more insight into your students' lives. And make sure you leave time for your students to share them. Trust me, they will want to! Plus, these are usually pretty funny, and it sets a great tone for often-difficult Friday classes.

A final key ingredient to each of these warmups is to allow students to share their thoughts with the class. When you show that you care about their ideas, students will pay you back by showing you that they care about yours. Respect is a two-way street.

Now you might be thinking that this sounds similar to how I started class for the first several years of my career. It is, after all, just having the students talk about non-content-related topics, right? While the general idea is similar, the process itself is *much* different. In the earlier scenario, I was a bystander, and there were a variety of separate conversations happening all at once. But in the new situation, I have become an active participant in the conversation, one that ideally includes the entire class. So rather than having ten mini-conversations happening all at once, the setting now looks like one cohesive discussion focused on a similar topic.

The purpose of this is to establish a sense of community where students know that you see them as more than just students. These two minutes that I spend talking with them person-to-person rather than teacher-to-student shows that I care about them beyond the content of my class. As a result of this deepened relationship, students are generally more willing to put forth their best effort (both academically and behaviorally) when that time comes. And here's the cool part: Those two minutes will more than pay for themselves over the course of each class. From my perspective, connecting with your students for two minutes early in the period in exchange for a better effort over the *remainder of your class* seems well worth the price.

As class winds down, I like to spend the last two minutes doing a cool-down where I recognize students who performed exceptionally well that day. (Please note that I do this after wrapping up the daily lesson and addressing any questions and/or homework concerns. I always try to make sure the first and last words out of my mouth are about them as people, not as students.) This usually involves me giving three shout-outs (along with a high five for each one) to students who participated in a manner that went above expectation. I may recognize when a student makes an insightful comment, helps another student, or simply says something that made me laugh.

After my three shout-outs, I open it up to the class to recognize up to three additional outstanding thoughts or actions they witnessed from their peers. Now before you say it, yes, the student shout-outs can be pretty hit-and-miss, depending on the class. That said, while the reasoning behind their shout-outs isn't always the most profound, the gesture itself further enhances an environment that is encouraging and supportive. And much like the learning done in class, the more they engage in this activity, the better they become at it.

WHAT YOU CAN DO TOMORROW

If you're looking to ease into this idea, here are five quick concepts that can be smoothly incorporated into any class.

- **GREET YOUR STUDENTS AT THE DOOR.** Greeting your students as they walk in the door is a simple way to start class in a positive direction. It shows students that you care and that you are excited to get the learning started.
- **TRY A WARMUP ACTIVITY.** When students walk in your room, have a warmup activity ready to go. Writing it on the board or telling students as they walk in is an easy way to get them working on this even before class starts.
- **LOOK FOR SMALL VICTORIES DURING CLASS.** Don't hold back on offering positive praise! A high five can be given out for even the smallest act. It's a quick, cheap, and effective way to keep students in a positive mindset during class.

- **CUSTOMIZE A HANDSHAKE.** To personalize this even more, some teachers go so far as to create customized handshakes for each student in the class. My personal favorites are the "slap, slap, bump" (slap hands forward, backward, followed by a fist bump), the "explosion" (fist bump that explodes afterwards), and the "upstairs/down-stairs" (high five that wraps all the way down to a low five in one fluid motion). And while I don't know the exact statistics behind it, I do know that everyone, *and I mean everyone,* enjoys a cool hand-shake or high five!

- **DO A COOL-DOWN SESSION.** At the end of class, give three shout-outs (and high fives) to your students. It will make them, and you, leave class feeling good!

A BLUEPRINT FOR FULL IMPLEMENTATION

Step 1: Get started as soon as possible.

I suggest implementing this concept at the start of the year, quarter, or semester. By using it early, it will provide time for students to really get into it. Additionally, it will give you the chance to establish a positive class culture right from the get-go.

Step 2: Be consistent in implementation.

Students thrive on routine, so it's important that you use this in a consistent manner. Doing it occasionally is similar to teaching a skill without a context—it usually doesn't stick. So figure out a plan that allows you to do it regularly. And if doing this daily seems overwhelming, maybe look at incorporating these ideas twice a week or on Fridays. Just make sure that whatever schedule you set up, you stick to it.

Step 3: Involve your students.

Listen to what your students are talking about, and use that information as the springboard for your warmups. If they are already invested in a topic, they will be more likely to share their thoughts when you bring it up. And the more they open up during the warmup and cool-down, the more likely they are to express their thoughts during class discussions. Similarly, the more they positively participate, the less likely they are to be a disruptive presence.

Step 4: Vary your topics and involve as many students as possible.

Make sure you address a wide range of topics during your warmups. The last thing you want to do is to consistently bring up a topic of interest to you and you alone. This hack is aimed at bringing everyone closer, so you'll want to make sure that as many people as possible are invested in what you're discussing. Also, make sure you include as many students as you can during the cool-down portion. And while you will probably have a few students who deserve a shout-out every day, don't overlook others. As a general rule, I try to make sure that each student in the class gets at least one shout-out every couple weeks. And yes, this is challenging, especially for *that* kid. That's why you'll want to recognize those positive moments when they happen.

Step 5: Always begin and end class on a positive note.

This is often the most challenging part of this hack, but it's important! No teaching up to the bell or yelling what the homework is as the class walks out the door! Your content gets the vast majority of your class time, so give this hack the time it needs to flourish. Even if it's as simple as saying "thank you" or "good job today," don't let the last words out of your mouth be about content.

OVERCOMING PUSHBACK

Time is a valuable commodity in schools, and asking teachers to give up four minutes every class period may raise some eyebrows. Here are some potential issues and how to deal with them.

I can't afford to give up class time for this. Yes, this is going to eat up four (maybe even five or six) minutes of your teaching time, but from my experience, easing your students in and out of class means they will work harder during the "teaching" portion. Meeting them at the door and starting class in a relaxing manner will jump-start them into performing at their highest levels.

This sounds like a lot of extra prep. While there is a little extra prep involved (such as finding the tip-of-the-week videos), most of the ideas in this hack can just happen organically based on what the students say. The majority of the concepts center on the students sharing, so all you really have to do is get the ball rolling.

My students won't participate in this. This is where picking the right warmup subject comes in. Choose topics that they *want* to talk about. And regarding the failures and haiku activities, I believe you will be surprised at how willing students are to create and share them. As for the cool-down, it's OK to let students be a little loose with their shout-outs. To me, this shows that they are comfortable in their environment, and that's kind of the point to all this.

My students don't do well with unstructured time. Let's be clear about this—this is not a free-for-all. Both the warmup and the cool-down are structured activities. You are leading both discussions from start to finish, and your students should be following the usual class rules and procedures. It's still organized—it's just not about content.

THE HACK IN ACTION

Fifth-grade teacher Sarah Button points out that she spends six-plus hours a day with her students, and that for any meaningful learning to take place, she has to know what makes her students tick. "What are their hobbies? What sports do they play? Who are my super readers? Who doesn't like reading? What instruments do they play? I really try to find out who my students are in the first few weeks of school, and I make sure to share my hobbies and interests with them as well. In my experience, once my students and I really get to know each other, the foundation is set for mutual respect and real learning can then begin," Button says.

An example of this "real learning" takes place every year during an annual writing contest where students are asked to write a letter to an author about how their book affected them personally. Button explains, "During the revision process for this contest, I offer students a serious dose of honest feedback with regard to their submissions. Generally speaking, this goes over well, and the writing dramatically improves. There was one student, however, who after receiving my feedback, struggled to understand my suggestions. She and her parents were initially quite upset about the recommendations that I had made, and she was hesitant to stray from her original ideas. But because of the positive and personal relationship that we had established throughout the year, she slowly started to embrace my recommendations. After a while, it seemed like the more we discussed her letter, the stronger our relationship became. Since that time, the student has reflected back numerous time about the critical feedback she received, and the family has returned to my classroom many times to reminisce about that defining moment in their daughter's learning."

Ms. Button concludes by saying, "I'm very clear with my students that I want to get to know and learn about them so that I can push and challenge them to do and be their best. This is where I find the joy of teaching—meeting these unique individuals, learning about them, and seeing them surpass their perceived limits. My students know that when I push them and have difficult conversations with them about the quality of their work or a social/behavior situation, it's because I care about them. And after they work through that frustration/problem, our class becomes an even stronger community."

From the minute your students walk into your class to the moment they leave, every second should be used to solidify the learning and the relationships. But the secret to this success lies in how you blend those two concepts together.

In the movie *Dangerous Minds,* new teacher LouAnne Johnson, a former Marine, entered her classroom armed with plenty of content knowledge but very little understanding of how classroom management worked. Slowly she began to realize that in order for learning to occur, she needed to connect with her students beyond the textbooks. She discovered that even the smallest act of kindness could make a lasting impression. Whether it was an impromptu karate lesson at the beginning of class, creating starter sentences based on of her students' lives, or making a Bob Dylan reference to emphasize a point, Ms. Johnson recognized that the best learning occurred only after her students knew that she cared about them as people. On any given day, she looked for small victories for which to praise her students, and she focused on their personal and academic growth more than test scores.

In order for any meaningful learning to take place *in* my class, I have to first form meaningful relationships *with* my class. It's surprising to discover that a fist bump or a shout-out can oftentimes mean a lot more to a student than the greatest of lesson plans. So don't be fooled; good things definitely can come in small packages.

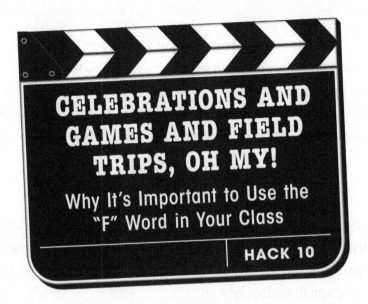

CELEBRATIONS AND GAMES AND FIELD TRIPS, OH MY!

Why It's Important to Use the "F" Word in Your Class

HACK 10

Never, ever underestimate the importance of having fun.
— RANDY PAUSCH, EDUCATOR

THE PROBLEM: TEACHERS ARE AFRAID TO HAVE FUN WITH THEIR CLASS

I'M NOT REALLY sure when it happened, but somewhere along the line, fun transformed itself into a concept that is often frowned upon in the classroom. It's like it has somehow become that other "F" word, and some teachers and administrators forbid its use within the walls of their schools. Students at every grade and in every subject are often denied the chance to, well, be kids at school. While the reasons themselves vary (high-stakes testing, overcrowded classrooms, scripted curriculums), the results don't. School is often a very boring place.

I maintain that one of the biggest contributing factors to student misconduct is boredom. Think about it. How often do you have students messing around when they are in the middle of doing something they enjoy? My guess is not very often. And that is why I argue that maintaining an appropriate level of fun in class plays a crucial role in creating a positive environment and improves the learning. Better behavior and improved learning as a result of having fun? Maybe the "F" word does have a place in your class.

THE HACK: CELEBRATIONS AND GAMES AND FIELD TRIPS, OH MY!

Do me a favor and take a minute (literally) to think about your favorite teachers and your favorite memories about them and their classes. This can be any teacher between kindergarten and high school graduation. Ready? Go!

If you are like me, the teachers and memories you just thought about are based more around fun and engagement than they are around content. See, no matter how much we try to fool ourselves, I doubt many of you thought, "Oh, I just loved the way Ms. Johnson talked about symbolism," or "Man, the way Mr. Charles explained the Pythagorean Theorem really got to me." (And just for the record, if you did think about those types of memories, you probably shouldn't admit it.)

 Classroom management is about a lot more than implementing rules; it's about understanding your students.

For me, I remember celebrating our basketball championship with an ice cream party in Ms. Ibsen's fifth-grade classroom. I think about playing a football-themed review game in Ms. Freeman's eighth-grade English class. And I still smile at the memory of finally bench-pressing more than Mr. Haggert during my eleventh-grade weightlifting class.

So while I'm sure that I learned a great deal from all of the teachers mentioned above, it's the fun we had *while learning* that sticks with me today. In addition, when I *really* think about it, those classes are also the ones where I behaved the best. The fact that I looked forward to going, and knowing that they would be interesting and engaging when I got there, kept me on my best behavior. The class itself was the classroom management! And that's why fun deserves a place within your class.

WHAT YOU CAN DO TOMORROW

Incorporating fun into the classroom doesn't have to be about bringing in balloons and throwing a huge celebration. In fact, small, frequent doses of fun are more effective for class morale and performance than the once-a-semester blowout bash. Here are a few ideas to shake things up that can be implemented immediately.

- **CREATE A BIRTHDAY BOARD/WALL.** While this sounds like a big undertaking, it's really quite simple. Section off part of your whiteboard and label it "This Month's Birthdays." Have students fill in their names with their birthdays and upcoming ages. When the day comes, let that student have unique privileges in class, like a special seat or a piece of candy. This only takes a second to acknowledge, and will have little (if any) impact on your lesson that day. But be warned: While singing happy birthday might sound like a good idea, by the time you've done it a few dozen times, it kind of loses its flavor.

If you want to do something beyond this, create a "Birthday Wall" where students have the option of bringing in a baby picture and hanging it up on the wall. And while I have them post their pictures and dates of birth on the wall, I don't have them write their names on these. Whenever a birthday rolls around, we try to guess whose big day it is. After figuring it out, implement your classroom's regular birthday privileges. Yes, this one will eat into a minute or two of your teaching time. The connections you make with students are more than worth it.

- **TELL A FUNNY STORY FROM YOUR CHILDHOOD.** Students love hearing stories from when you were their age, so if you can link a childhood story to your lesson, take advantage of it. And even if you can't relate it to your lesson, use opportunities to share these stories when they arise. For me, I have a Halloween story that makes an appearance every year, and the same holds true after the first snow-fall of winter. And while neither of these is necessarily content-related, they do serve as a great change of pace from the status quo.

Another twist on this idea is to model how to do a show-and-tell with your students. You can demonstrate what this looks like by bringing in an item that holds meaning for you and explaining why it's important. This can then lead to students holding a weekly show-and-tell where three or four students do a one-minute presentation on items that are important to them.

• **HAVE STUDENTS SHARE A FEW JOKES.** As a way to relieve stress prior to a big test, I often allow my students a chance to share a few jokes with the class. You will obviously want to establish parameters for these jokes, but there is usually a student or two who has a good one ready to share. This is also an excellent opportunity for you to connect with your students by offering up a teacher joke or two. The cheesier the better!

• **PLAY BINGO.** Creating a class-themed game of BINGO is sure to engage all of your students! I generally mix up the squares to include topics that are academic, social, and personal. These are a great way to reinforce any skills taught in class while also fostering a positive student/teacher relationship. I often use these for summer reading assignments, but they could easily be adapted to review a unit or prepare for a test. (See Act 10: BINGO.)

As a way to help you grow personally, academically, and socially, please complete the BINGO board.

Full credit for five in a row. Surprise for all students who complete the entire sheet!

Learn a new joke	Try eating a food you've never had before	Help make dinner for your family	Go six straight hours (during daylight hours) without using technology	Text three friends about your summer reading books
Watch a YouTube video about something that interests you	Clean your room once a week for the entire summer	Draw something	Write your summer reading paper	Go to the zoo, a museum, a national park, the Planetarium, or the aquarium
Spend a day outside playing with family or friends	Snapchat a selfie with a summer reading book to someone in the grade	FREE SPACE	Do the laundry at your house (get help if you have never done this before)	Read a book besides the one assigned for summer reading
Do the dishes/load and unload the dishwasher five times	Edit/revise your summer reading paper	Snapchat, text, or become Facebook friends with someone at school outside your friend group	Watch/Go to a movie and talk about it with someone after	Take out the garbage at your house at least once a week for the entire summer
Make your bed for a week straight	Listen to a cool Podcast about something that interests you	Finish your summer reading book	Write a short poem about something you do this summer	Do five random acts of kindness

Behind the Scenes Act 10: BINGO

- **DRAW SOMETHING.** I am a terrible artist, and yet at the same time, I love to draw. In fact, most students, from the stick-figure cartoonist to the perfectly scaled artist, enjoy busting out the colored pencils every now and then. There are all kinds of ways to get students to draw (draw their vocab words, summarize a reading, explain a concept) that can enhance the topic at hand. Plus, drawing can calm a class down in a way that is engaging and fun.

- **TAKE A SELFIE.** Students love taking selfies, so find a way to use this to your advantage! Birthday selfies (with me and the person celebrating the birthday) have become a regular part of my class routine, and students really enjoy the recognition. Additionally, there are lots of other ways to incorporate selfies into the classroom that will help foster a strong relationship with your students. Snap a selfie if you and a student happen to be dressed alike or if you're wearing similar Halloween costumes. Use selfies as part of a BINGO game. Plus, selfies can easily be printed and hung around the room. Selfies are an easy way to connect with your students in a silly, yet harmless, manner.

A BLUEPRINT FOR FULL IMPLEMENTATION

Step 1: Look for ways to add fun into what you already do.

Having fun should be used to supplement the learning, not replace it. Too much fun is just as bad (if not worse) as not enough. No need to create hour-long sessions of fun; instead, find a spot or two every day where you can add in a little more amusement.

Step 2: Incorporate new activities into your class.

A few ideas that work with any grade or subject include:

- A quick YouTube video can spice up any lesson (see Hack 5).

- Review games always get students fired up. And try to go beyond the traditional "Jeopardy" review. Pictionary, Kahoot, charades, and any game that involves shooting a ball into the garbage can are always big hits in my class. The more interactive the better!

- Read a children's book aloud that emphasizes the skill or concept you're studying. This works regardless of the grade or subject. Plus, if you're looking to settle a group down, read them a story and watch the craziness melt out of the room.

- Need more ideas? Check out Hack 9 for more fun and engaging ideas.

Step 3: Have mini-celebrations!

If you look for them, there are all kinds of reasons to celebrate in class. Birthdays. Holidays. Team championships. Winter break.

Spring break. The list goes on! The opportunities are there. The question is, are you willing to give up a minute or two to celebrate them?

Step 4: Plan field trips and bring in guest speakers.

As much as students love coming to your class, they love *not* coming to your class even more! Field trips are a great way to enhance the learning via an experiential adventure. And these don't have to be all-day escapades. Some quick-trip ideas include the park, the zoo, local museums, the courthouse, and the police station. Trips like these can often be cross curricular in nature, and blending in a little collaboration never hurts. Don't have the money to take your class on a trip? Then bring the info to the class courtesy of a guest speaker! While musicians and authors are awesome, they often come with a hefty price tag. If you are willing to put in a little elbow grease, there are local experts like judges, police officers, and doctors who are often willing to volunteer their insights.

Step 5: Include downtime in the mix.

Don't you love those rare occasions when you get a couple of free minutes to just relax? Sometimes even a few minutes of relaxation is enough to jump-start the old system! And the same holds true with your students. Look for little ways that you can take some of the daily pressure off students. What about a Monday meditation session to start class? Or how about homework-free Wednesdays? There are numerous opportunities to give your students a break, and if you plan for them, the "lost" content time will be replaced by their increased productivity while working.

OVERCOMING PUSHBACK

Is fun a necessary part of school? No, it isn't. Will your class be more inviting and student-oriented if you incorporate more fun into your daily routine? You better believe it! But old habits die hard, and for those who think fun should happen outside the weekday hours of 7:30 a.m. to 3:30 p.m., here are some thoughts.

I don't have time for fun during class. Classroom management is about a lot more than implementing rules; it's about understanding your students. If you work students too hard for too long, burnout or kickback is bound to happen. By adding in a daily dose of fun, you will keep your students engaged in the learning, with an added bonus of more stable behavior as a result of letting out some of the pressure from the daily stress of school.

This sounds like a lot of work. There really isn't a way to deny this one when it comes to the bigger ideas like field trips and guest speakers. And while it will take extra work to crank up the fun, the majority of these ideas are fairly simple and inexpensive. The payoff is that your students will enjoy class more, behave better, and learn more in the process. It will make your day more interesting, too!

What if my students get inappropriate with their jokes and stories? This is why you establish clear guidelines. Many classroom management issues happen partly because the teacher provided unclear expectations, so if you want this idea to be successful, make sure all your students understand what is *and is not* acceptable. If you help them understand that opportunities like these are a privilege, they will be more likely to respect the boundaries.

THE HACK IN ACTION

At South Bonneville Jr. High in the mid 1980s, Mrs. Rowberry's room was the place to be! In the mornings, she would open her classroom early so we could hang out. At lunch, after chowing down our food, we would head to her room and draw pictures on her chalkboard. And during class, well, that's when things *really* got interesting.

I remember her telling us stories about her childhood. She also gave us a few minutes each week to share the latest (appropriate) joke we had heard. I think of the times she had her husband come to class and play songs for us on his guitar, and us making up geography lyrics based on some of the most popular songs of the time. And more than anything else, I remember wanting to impress her, because I didn't want to be the reason that the fun would end. So while it was fun that drew me in, it was my respect for her that kept me in check.

Current high school junior Sydney Young understands the connection that Mrs. Rowberry made with her students, and she sees the benefits that come from weaving fun into the daily curriculum. "Fun related to the material, such as watching a video, hearing jokes, or getting on a tangent all feel like off-task fun, but actually lead me to make new connections, enjoy the material, and spend time processing the information. The best classes I've had blended the curriculum with a perfect combination of fun and mini-celebrations, and it's that combination that led me to be successful that class," Young says.

She adds that the value that comes from these experiences runs much deeper than simply gaining a better understanding of the content. "During these activities and celebrations, I connect with students I might not normally speak with, which increases my confidence about participating in discussions or presenting because I feel as though I am amongst a large group of friends."

Mrs. Rowberry knew how to use the "F" word in her class, and Sydney sees its benefit from the student perspective as well. Are you willing to add the "F" word to your class?

In *School of Rock,* Dewey Finn took this concept of creating fun in the classroom to heart during his stint as a substitute teacher. Whether he was taking his class on a field trip to the Battle of the Bands, incorporating a new activity by teaching the "Math is a Wonderful Thing" song, or modeling his passion for music by playing alongside his class, Mr. S. (as he is called in the movie) made sure to sprinkle a touch of fun into every aspect of class.

The success of his method is best illustrated halfway through the movie when his student Freddy asks, "Are we gonna be goofing off every day?" While the knee-jerk reaction might be negative, the hidden beauty of this statement is that while Freddy interpreted what they had been doing as messing around, it actually was an effective teaching strategy that mixed collaboration, self-direction, and fun amongst the learning outcomes. And as evidenced by the class participation in the final Battle of the Bands performance, the method resulted in a class full of students who were learning while enjoying class at the same time.

In today's time-crunched, test-driven schools, having fun in the classroom is becoming harder to accomplish each day. But with just a little effort and planning on our part as teachers, we can bring it back. We all want our classrooms to be places where students like to be. We all want our students to be more engaged in the learning.

SHHH...THE MOVIE'S ABOUT TO BEGIN!

CONCLUSION

AFTER NEARLY TWENTY years of teaching, this has become clear to me: Understanding the content of your class is the easiest part of being a teacher. The hardest? Well, that's classroom management. I say this because regardless of how well you know the ins and outs of your subject area, it doesn't amount to much if you can't get your students interested in what you are saying and doing. And that's why building strong relationships with your students is the key factor in creating a positive learning environment.

Every hack presented here centers around the bond you form with your students both inside and outside the walls of your classroom. These relationships serve as the foundation from which everything revolves—from content to classroom management. Teaching is hard, and there are a lot of good teachers out there who show up each day, adequately teach their classes, and then head home.

But you didn't take all those education classes hoping that one day you could become an *average* teacher. And you don't continually participate in professional development opportunities with the goal that you can turn into a *slightly better* educator. Finally, you don't keep up with all the latest educational trends *on your free time* praying that they will help you become a *mediocre* teacher. Nah, you want more that that! You want to be the best teacher that you can be—for both yourself and your students. It's one thing to be a good teacher; it's another to be the type of teacher they make movies about! The fact that you picked up this book shows that you have the desire to become one of those teachers, and now you have the strategies to make it happen.

I truly believe that teaching is the greatest job in the world, and each one of us, regardless of who, what, or where we teach, has the opportunity to changes lives *every single day.* It is my hope that the ideas and examples presented here will help you accomplish that.

SNEAK PEEK

TEACH COLLABORATION SKILLS
Harness dissonance to enhance learning

The surest way to corrupt a youth is to instruct
him to hold in higher esteem those who think
alike than those who think differently.
— FRIEDRICH NIETZSCHE, PHILOSOPHER

THE PROBLEM: STUDENTS DO NOT
KNOW HOW TO COLLABORATE

A s a classroom teacher, coach, and administrator, Erin has heard teachers in various settings complain about students' inabilities to successfully work together in a group. "What have you tried to remedy that problem?" she often asks. The most common responses range from adding a group work component to a rubric, creating a divide-and-conquer method, or simply nothing at all.

Let's dissect the most common responses:

- Adding a group work component to a rubric: Is this rubric being used to give your students a score? If the answer to that question is yes, then you are potentially committing educational malpractice. As educators, we certainly should not be giving a grade for something we have not taught.

If the rubric is being used exclusively to provide formative feedback, then you may be onto something.

- Creating a divide-and-conquer method: Allowing students to continually jigsaw their projects is sending the message this is how collaboration works. Essentially, this practice gives students the permission to take their ball and go home when confronted with an uncomfortable group dynamic, rather than working through the challenge with their team.

- Nothing at all: Completely ignoring collaboration is sending the message it is not important. Students learn to value experiences that receive attention and feedback. By failing to address collaboration, the importance of the skill diminishes.

According to the National Association of Colleges and Employers Job Outlook 2016 survey, 78.5% of respondents identified "ability to work on a team" as an essential skill looked for in new hires. The ability to work on a team, collaboration, was rated higher than all other skills (communication, work ethic, initiative, etc.) with the exception of leadership, which was rated marginally higher at 80%.

Why then, do we continue to overlook this crucial skill in our classrooms? Sure, we provide opportunities for students to collaborate, but how do we prepare them for these opportunities, and what happens when they go wrong?

We simply do not have enough time to do everything, which is why we need to be insanely picky about how we allocate this precious resource. Taking the time to teach collaboration skills in your classroom is an investment in the future work you expect from your students. When students engage in collaboration, their thinking is elevated and an active learning experience is created.

THE HACK: TEACH COLLABORATION SKILLS

The common responses shared in the previous section suggest we lack a shared vision for collaboration. What exactly should collaboration look like, sound like, and feel like in our classrooms? Teams of educators could spend hours, or even days, debating, constructing, or wordsmithing a specific definition. Merriam-Webster defines collaboration as "to work with another person or group in order to achieve or do something." This definition includes the major facets essential for our students:

- "with another person"—This is where the divide-and conquer method fails; it confuses collaboration with efficiency. Working with someone requires dialogue and productive struggle, even for our youngest students. Friction is the key to creating a quality outcome. We are remiss if we are not demonstrating for our students how to use dissonance for reflection and refinement.

- "achieve or do something"—Collaboration should lead to something, not always a tangible product, but something. What is the purpose? What is the common goal? We will discuss creating a motivating common goal in Hack 4, but establishing this something is key to creating a collaborative team. If we expect students to collaborate, we must teach them how. This explicit instruction goes beyond kindergarten lessons on learning to share and truly transcends grade level.

WHAT YOU CAN DO TOMORROW

- Pre-assess. It is imperative that you do not make assumptions about students' abilities to collaborate based on their age or the types of classes in which they are enrolled. To determine where you need to start with your instruction on collaboration, pre-assess your class. You can gather this information by asking your students to reflect on past experiences or by observing students while they work together.

- Curate. Locate examples of collaborative experiences. A quick Google search will return an abundance of videos you can use as exemplars. Curate resources such as YouTube clips from popular sitcoms or education-specific videos found on the Teaching Channel to immerse your students in dialogue about collaboration. While doing so, students can uncover what effective collaboration should and should not look like in the classroom.

- Collaborate. When was the last time you engaged in a quality, collaborative experience? The next time you are in a planning meeting or workshop, tune into the collaborative skills used by those in the room. These skills may include: discussion skills, body language, transitions, organization strategies, etc. You will have more to offer your students if you are well versed in collaboration.

A BLUEPRINT FOR FULL IMPLEMENTATION

Step 1: Define and model what collaboration looks like.

It is best to start with what collaboration looks like because it is the easiest feature to observe. Students should watch the videos you curated or visit another classroom currently engaged in a collaborative experience. Ask your students to note what they see happening. It may be helpful to break students into groups and have each group observe a different element. Good elements to observe are: body language, materials, environment, and location.

When collaborating face-to-face, we use certain body language that allows our partner(s) to know we are engaged. We lean in, uncross our arms, and make eye contact. These behaviors are not always natural, so we need to demonstrate and practice with our students. We also need to model for students the appropriate ways to use their mobile devices (laptops, phones, etc.), so they enhance rather than distract from collaborative experiences. Students will need to build their work-focused stamina. Adolescents especially need to practice filtering out the static from their environment to fully engage with the human beings with whom they are working.

BUY
HACKING PROJECT BASED LEARNING

AVAILABLE AT:
Amazon.com
10Publications.com
and bookstores near you

More from
TIMES 10 PUBLICATIONS

Browse all titles at 10Publications.com

Hacking School Discipline
9 Ways to Create a Culture of Empathy & Responsibility Using Restorative Justice
By Nathan Maynard and Brad Weinstein

Reviewers proclaim this *Washington Post* Bestseller to be "maybe the most important book a teacher can read, a must for all educators, fabulous, a game changer!" Teachers and presenters Nathan Maynard and Brad Weinstein demonstrate how to eliminate punishment and build a culture of responsible students and independent learners in a book that will become your new blueprint for school discipline. Twelve straight months at #1 on Amazon and still going strong, *Hacking School Discipline* is disrupting education like nothing we've seen in decades—maybe centuries.

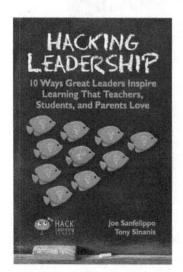

Hacking Leadership
10 Ways Great Leaders Inspire Learning That Teachers, Students, and Parents Love
By Joe Sanfelippo and Tony Sinanis

Renowned school leaders Joe Sanfelippo and Tony Sinanis bring readers inside schools that few stakeholders have ever seen—places where students not only come first, but have a unique voice in teaching and learning. The authors ignore the bureaucracy that stifles many leaders, focusing instead on building a culture of engagement, transparency, and most importantly, fun. *Hacking Leadership* has superintendents, principals, and teachers around the world employing strategies they never before believed possible.

Browse all titles at 10Publications.com

Project Based Learning
Real Questions. Real Answers. How to Unpack PBL and Inquiry
By Ross Cooper and Erin Murphy

Educators would love to leverage project based learning to create learner-centered opportunities for their students, but why isn't PBL the norm? Because teachers have questions. *Project Based Learning* is Ross Cooper and Erin Murphy's response to the most common and complex questions educators ask about PBL and inquiry, including: How do I structure a PBL experience? How do I get grades? How do I include direct instruction? What happens when kids don't work well together? Learn how to teach with PBL and inquiry in any subject or grade.

Even More Hacking Engagement
50 New Ways to Make Learning Fun for All Students
By James Alan Sturtevant

If you and your students aren't approaching your class each day with excitement for the new ideas and learning surprises you're about to experience, then it's time to hack your student engagement.

This four-decade veteran classroom teacher knows how to engage learners, and he's sharing his best ideas with you. Author James Sturtevant wrote *Hacking Engagement* and *Hacking Engagement Again*, and now he's back with 50 new ways to make the classroom fun for everyone. You can implement these tips and tools starting tomorrow! When you apply Sturtevant's strategies, your class will become the one they don't want to miss. It's time to engage.

Browse all titles at 10Publications.com

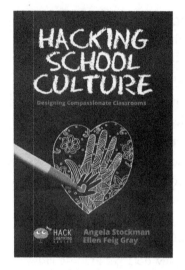

Hacking School Culture
Designing Compassionate Classrooms
By Angela Stockman and Ellen Feig Gray

Bullying prevention and character-building programs are deepening our awareness of how today's kids struggle and how we might help, but many agree: they aren't enough to create school cultures where students and staff flourish. This inspired Angela Stockman and Ellen Feig Gray to seek out systems and educators who were getting things right and share their findings in this insightful book.

Be Excellent on Purpose
Intentional Strategies for Impactful Leadership
By Sanée Bell

Excellence is a journey where one discovers who they are, what they value, and the principles that drive them. But it's not always easy for educators to rise above the fray and live a purposeful life. To *Be Excellent on Purpose* means making a plan for life and working the plan to make it a reality. In this inaugural book in the Lead Forward Series, teacher, author, presenter, and school leader Sanée Bell shares personal and professional stories and strategies that will make your leadership intentional and impactful.

Resources from Times 10

10Publications.com

Nurture your inner educator:
10publications.com/educatortype

Podcasts:
hacklearningpodcast.com
jamesalansturtevant.com/podcast

On Twitter:
@10Publications
@HackMyLearning
#Times10News
#RealPBL
@LeadForward2
#LeadForward
#HackLearning
#HackingLeadership
#MakeWriting
#HackingQs
#HackingSchoolDiscipline
#LeadWithGrace
#HackingSchoolLibraries

All things Times 10:
10Publications.com

MEET THE AUTHOR

 **Mike Roberts** has taught middle school English for the past twenty years. In that time, he has received numerous awards, including the 2014 Utah English Teacher of the Year. Beyond the classroom, he has been a featured speaker at dozens of state, regional, and national conferences. He has served on many educational committees, and he was a featured columnist in *English Journal,* where he shared his insights on using YA literature in the classroom. Additionally, he co-authored *The New Science Teacher's Handbook: What You Didn't Learn From Student Teaching.* Beyond his middle school teaching, Mike also teaches college classes focused on classroom management and literacy in the content areas. He loves sharing his ideas with others, and he always feels honored when people actually show up to hear him speak. When he's not teaching or presenting, Mike can usually be found running ultramarathons in the mountains. And even after all these years, he's still not sure which takes more energy ... a week with eighth graders or running a hundred-mile race.

You can follow Mike on Twitter @BaldRoberts.

ACKNOWLEDGEMENTS

WHILE IT MIGHT be my name on the cover of this book, there are a ton of people who helped make this book a reality. First, I'd like to acknowledge all the teachers and students who were so willing to share their experiences and thoughts with me. It is their insight that brings the essence of this book to life. Next, I'd like to thank my mom and my kids for everything they have added to my life over the years. Third, a special shout-out goes to Sarah, my biggest supporter, who has always been there to help me hammer out a sentence or offer up a suggestion. Along those same lines, I would be remiss if I didn't acknowledge my appreciation to Mark Barnes (and the entire Hack Learning team) for taking a chance on a middle school English teacher. And finally to my grandma, for always pushing me to do a better job today than I did yesterday.

X10

TIMES 10 provides practical solutions that busy educators can read today and use tomorrow. We bring you content from experienced teachers and leaders, and we share it through books, podcasts, webinars, articles, events, and ongoing conversations on social media. Our books and materials help turn practice into action. Stay in touch with us at 10Publications.com and follow our updates on Twitter @10Publications and #Times10News.

Made in United States
North Haven, CT
20 August 2024

56352399R00098